The
Psychic
Handbook

The
Psychic
Handbook

Betty F. Balcombe

ⓐ**WEISER BOOKS**
Boston, MA/York Beach, ME

First published in 2000 by
Red Wheel/Weiser, LLC
York Beach, ME
With offices at
368 Congress Street
Boston, MA 02210
www.redwheelweiser.com

08 07 06 05 04
10 9 8 7 6 5 4 3

Library of Congress Cataloging-in-Publication Data
Balcombe, Betty F.
    The Psychic Handbook / Betty F. Balcombe
        p.   cm.
    Includes index.
    ISBN 1-57863-213-7
    1. Psychic ability. 2. Psychics—United States
  3. Balcombe, Betty F.   I. Title.
BF1031.B226   1995
133.8—dc20   95-3102
                                          CIP

Printed in the United States of America
CCP

Dedicated to Douglas H Balcombe
for his love, care and support

Contents

Introduction

I am psychic and have spent most of my adult life healing, psychic reading and teaching. I teach psychic development and spiritual awareness, sharing my experience, knowledge and insight in an endeavour to remove fear from a natural and normal ability to give and receive energy; and also to raise the standard and understanding of psychic work.

I delayed writing about my psychic and spiritual beliefs as I believed that teachers and seekers learn from debate and the exchange of views and information. Written words can become fixtures, and the reader runs the risk of absorbing without thought and selection. But those who studied with me felt they could benefit from having the basis of the teachings and beliefs available in book form, to use as a reference and as a refresher course. They asked me to write it for them.

The news travelled and I received requests from people who had heard of me, but were not able to join the groups, that the book be expanded to include them. I then wrote in more detail, to facilitate understanding.

It was brought to my notice that many people, not psychic but spiritually aware, were interested in my beliefs. And there were others who had a very strange and frightened view of the world of the psychic, and who needed a logical, caring base from which to reappraise the subject.

This book is the result. It is not intended as a comprehensive instruction manual and cannot possibly answer all questions. But if you choose to read it, I hope it will stimulate your thinking and remove fear by helping you to understand.

Fear is the great destroyer; knowledge is the bridge to understanding. Open your eyes — there is nothing to fear, and you may be surprised.

Betty F Balcombe

PART ONE

Being
psychic

This chapter relates to people who know they are psychic and those who are not sure. It seeks to clarify what a psychic is, and gives information and exercises to develop and learn control of the ability to give healing energy and readings. It also gives exercises in balance and harmony.

What is a psychic?

As a young child I found I had an ability to 'see' colours and energies. I also 'knew' about other people and could feel a healing energy transfer from myself to them if they were in need. Gradually I came to the awareness that these abilities were not common to all and later I came to realise that I was in fact what is known as 'a psychic'.

A psychic is a person who has the ability to sense information from other people through the aura energy which surrounds us all. The aura is your record of all that you have experienced and are likely to experience whilst on earth, plus a link to your soul, which incorporates a record of all that has occurred since its creation. This information can be sensed by you if you're psychic as pictures, words, feelings, smells or a feeling of 'knowing'. The more practised the psychic is in sensing and understanding what is received, the more help he or she can give to others to help themselves.

As I've already mentioned, psychics also possess healing energy, which can be transferred to anyone in need.

The sensing ability and healing energy of psychics causes them to seem different from other people, and it is this energy difference which can set them apart and cause others to be afraid of them. If we were all psychic we would all have this energy and it would not feel strange; there would be no problem of acceptance. However, not everyone is psychic, so it is not natural to all. Over the ages people who possessed this different energy have been praised, honoured, revered, hounded, feared and destroyed, their acceptance within society depending on the needs, knowledge and awareness of their contemporaries.

The strength of, and ability to use, psychic energy varies from person to person. Some psychics are able to sense and interpret information, transmit healing energy and diagnose illness and its cause. Others, sometimes unaware of their psychic ability, are drawn to the creative and communicative areas of life – music, art and acting. Others are attracted to the health professions or become politicians and religious leaders, preferring to communicate through voice. Some believe their difference from others has singled them out for special work.

But this 'difference' has its down side. Even in a liberal, open-minded society it is often hard for those of us with psychic abilities to fit in. Young psychics, for instance, can feel out of place in their family. Usually he or she is the 'odd one out' and feels alone. Many feel so out of contact with the other family members that they believe they must be adopted. As they grow, their 'differences' can become more apparent; at school they find it hard to play with other children, who may ignore, reject or torment them. Some psychic children, however, take the bull by the horns and become playground gang leaders, desperately finding exciting things to do in order to keep ahead, and therefore safe. In adult life this can develop into a need to be a leader.

It can seem that psychic ability is physically inherited, but, in my opinion, it is not; it is part of the soul. I believe that as a psychic, you are always psychic. You will have had psychic ability in each life lived and will have used it in different ways. The impression that psychic ability is inherited comes about because some are born into families where the ability is already known and accepted, which is a great help in integration.

Psychics are ultra-sensitive. Many suffer great trials and pain, both physical and emotional, especially in their younger years. These experiences provide invaluable knowledge which can be used in helping others, but they are hard to bear at the time. Understanding often comes with hindsight. Psychic, can be extremely emotional and vulnerable. Many feel they are different, but do not always know why. This can undermine confidence. I have found that many learn at a very young age to be careful about what they say, and can appear arrogant, cold or haughty in their desire to survive without revealing their vulnerability. They are often confused and confusing, as they can get involved in many different creative activities. A creative psychic might appear totally dedicated to painting, then suddenly switch to sculpture, then on to writing and finally get involved in music. In later life, however, he or she might do none of these activities, being content merely to watch and listen. Psychics usually give 100 per cent of themselves to everything they do, often becoming listless and disillusioned when ending a particular creative phase. They need to be the best they possibly can and allow themselves no half-measures.

Many active psychics use their ability to help other people through healing and giving readings and messages. A psychic can sense the potential, opportunities and obstacles projected by a person, who can then choose whether or not to change the path he or she is on. But some psychics do not dissociate from personal traits and these can interfere. For instance, a psychic who is pessimistic could relate what he or she receives pessimistically, whereas an optimist could relate optimistically. Both would be allowing their own personality to change what they have received. This should be carefully corrected. As a psychic I believe you should disconnect from your own personality and relate clearly and precisely what you sense, relating all choices to the person you are helping so that he or she can choose which path to follow.

On occasions psychics can sense information about another person, who is known or unknown to them, without that person's knowledge or request. When this happens to me, for example, I immediately move away and/or think about everyday matters. The only time a psychic should give a message to a person is when it is requested or permission is given. To go to a person and give them messages and personal information without their request is unethical, intrusive and egotistical. If as a psychic you are to achieve a high quality of work, professionalism and accuracy, you must learn control (see p.17).

Using psychic abilities in a 'reading' or healing session enables the psychic to find the cause of distress, and help clients to understand themselves by giving them information they may not have been aware of previously. They can then choose whether or not to change the path they are on.

Some psychic messages received can seem incorrect when the event foretold does not occur. This happens when the person has changed his or her direction and chosen a different path from that sensed and commented on by the psychic. It is helpful, therefore, if all opportunities are sensed and related. If the psychic senses trouble ahead he or she can sense why it is there and if and how it can be avoided, changed or worked through.

The wider a psychic's life experience, the better he or she can interpret what is sensed from people. A psychic who has not acquired knowledge of life personally will be limited in the help he or she can give others in psychic work. In fact such psychics can cause great distress by their inability to understand and communicate what they are sensing.

However, all is not lost: psychics can improve the psychic energy link, and with practice their ability can become sharper and more accurate. It is a good rule if you are going to work as a psychic to use methods which feel natural and work for you, and reject the ones which you find difficult or unacceptable.

The rest of the chapter contains general assistance and advice to enable you to make the best use of your psychic abilities and to achieve the right kind of relationship with those who seek help from you.

Comfort and control

Psychics have enough healing energy within their aura to cover all their personal needs and to help on a general level with other living things. When coming into contact with anyone or anything in need of help or healing, your spirit automatically connects to its soul energy and more healing energy begins to flow through you to the needy person or situation.

Psychic energy is a part of the soul and is self-replenishing. When a session with a person is complete you may find you need to switch down, as the energy can continue to flow after the person has left. This could cause you distress. There are two main areas in which psychics can feel discomfort: the centre of the forehead and the nape of the neck.

When the flow of energy does not slow down, you can be left feeling bright and energised, and can overload – rather like a light bulb which, instead of being switched off when not needed, is left burning. Eventually it will either fade out or explode. The excess energy can also cause one to feel depressed, lethargic or apathetic or to experience intense mental irritation and short temper. It is essential to control the flow of energy when work is over. A symbolic action, chosen by you as your 'on and off switch' (for example stroking your nose) is all that is needed. Gently stroking the mid-forehead area is also beneficial. Some may find the image of glowing lights around them, which can be turned down, helpful.

Many psychics, I find, are badly affected by excessive movement. Jarring the body through activities such as jogging can cause the spine to go into stress and affect the neck area. As the nape of the neck is very vulnerable, jarring the spine can cause extreme pain in the back, neck and head. Psychics need rhythmic movement: swimming, cycling, smooth running and steady walking are all beneficial. Many do not like competitive sport and tend to be found exercising alone or only competing when their chance of winning is very high. There is a natural tendency to conserve energy, and we do not usually like movement unless there is a good reason!

Psychics should take care not to over-enthuse. When in company and the subject arises, it is fine to join in and give an opinion, but not to give a lecture! When questions are being asked, I find it is wise to answer the question asked and no more. Giving too much information to a person who is not ready for it, and cannot handle it, will cause various reactions. Some people, for instance, will walk away in mid-sentence, while others may change the subject abruptly or take one sentence of little importance and make an argument of it. Some may ask more questions, showing an interest in the subject. Many questions can be answered by another question, so that the questioner realises he or she had the answer all along. They may decide to seek information from other sources to find their own way of growing. No one is right about everything for everybody. Always be prepared to listen.

Water is essential to the well-being and harmony of a psychic. Ideally you should live near a natural water source such as the sea, river, stream, lake or pond. Most psychics find they live near water having been drawn to it naturally. The water keeps the air moistened and you can be harmonised and inspired by watching its changing patterns.

When healing and psychic work are finished for the day, psychics should close off from the energy flow they have attracted for their patients. The symbolic switchdown mentioned above is sometimes sufficient, but to make sure the following exercise can be carried out. It switches us down, clears our aura and protects our solar centre.

 ## Switchdown exercise after work

Stand with your feet slightly apart, your elbows level with your shoulders, and your hands level with the side of your head, palms facing inward. Bring your hands together in front of your forehead and bring them down slowly together, passing all the centres, to the creativity centre. Bring your arms and hands back to the shoulder position and place your palms together at mid-forehead. Then take them, still together, over the top of your head, down the nape of your neck and then off at the shoulders. Bring your hands to waist level and pass them over each other, stroke downwards over the lower body. Brush down each leg and under each foot and shake your body.

By carrying out this exercise, the energy will be controlled and will become sufficient for your personal needs. It will clear the aura, balance the centres and regulate mood patterns.

Psychics who go into crowded areas automatically tune into extra energy. It is a good idea to use the exercise above before entering a crowded place and again when leaving.

 ## To replenish flagging energy levels

1 Half fill a glass with liquid: boiled, cooled water is best. Encircle the glass with your hands, fingers touching. Stare at the liquid for approximately ten seconds, sensing colours

entering; sometimes it will bubble. Drink the energised liquid. This can give you up to four hours' extra energy.

2 Alternatively stand, feet slightly apart, relaxed, with your arms stretched out sideways slightly higher than your shoulders. Pause, and slowly bring your hands together to rest on your solar plexus. Now stretch your arms out slightly below shoulder level, pause, and bring your hands back to rest on your solar plexus, stretch your arms out and, pointing down to the ground, pause, then bring your hands together to rest on the solar plexus. Pause for ten seconds. The energy derived from this exercise can last up to three hours.

These exercises gather your own totally harmless reserve energies from your aura field and replace them in your centres. They will only work once at any given time, and if you are so fatigued that you have used up all your reserve aura energy already they will have no effect.

Psychics do not always switch down easily at the end of their day. You can feel very bright and finely tuned, and on some occasions your brain seems to be boiling. The following suggestions will help you sleep.

 ## End-of-day routine

Prepare for bed an hour before time. Play soft music, avoid watching TV or listening to animated conversations or debates. Go over what has occurred during the day. It helps to write or record disturbing thoughts for attention another time. Prepare a drink and place it by the bed. Make sure you are warm. Lie down, and sense colours gently rippling through you. Slowly breathe in; as you breathe out feel peace and stillness in your head, gently soothing and calming the mind. Breathe in again and, as you breathe out, feel peace and calmness entering your body. Continue breathing rhythmically in this way through your body and finish below your feet. Should you still be awake when you reach this point, which is unlikely, repeat the exercise. Many people wake during the night on their return from an out-of-body trip or a special dream. When this happens the body dehydrates and they wake up. Sip the liquid you placed near your bed, and your body will relax again and go back to sleep.

Self-healing

Psychic or not, we all need to energise and balance our centres each day. The following exercise can be carried out every morning. It energises the body, pinpoints imbalanced areas and enables us to attend to our own well-being.

Morning energising exercise
On waking, and whilst still in a relaxed state, check each part of your body. Note any part which is not at ease. Breathe in, and as you breathe out, concentrate on your big toe, feel it coming alive — feel the blood flowing inside, feel it getting warm. Move along to the next toe and the next, concentrating on each in turn. Wriggle all your toes. Concentrate on your foot, feeling the blood, bones and skin warm and alive. Continue up the leg. When you reach the knee, bend your leg, flex the muscles. When you reach the top of your leg return to the other big toe and repeat the process to the top of that leg.

Now concentrate on the body, the organs, the intestines. Breathe in, feel the lungs expanding, feel the heart beating. Flex the back muscles and check the spine.

When you reach the shoulders, concentrate on an arm — remember to move all joints when you reach them. Flex the wrist, spread the hand and the fingers, flex the muscles. Go to the other shoulder and repeat. The neck is next; it is movable, so move it.

Now activate the head, starting with the face. Move your jaw, puff out your cheeks, poke out your tongue, wrinkle your nose, sniff the air, roll your eyes, stretch your brows. Listen in order to activate your ears, concentrate on your brain, sense outside the head and notice how your hair sits like a cap on your head.

Concentrate on a spot just above the top of your head — you may sense a colour, or else a beautiful colourful place. As you watch the image, one colour will stand out from the rest. This is the colour you need for the day. Your aura needs this colour. Put your hands on areas which feel imbalanced and feel the colour pulsating through your hands into the area. Whilst transferring the colour, try to sense why the imbalance has occurred.

Should the discomfort return during the day, through your hands, put the same colour in the area and it will be relieved.

Some mornings you may have found that the clothes you put on that day felt very uncomfortable. This was because you had chosen a colour which was not in harmony with your energy needs, and your aura was desperately seeking a colour to balance itself. By finding your colour through the exercise just described, you will save time and energy going through your entire wardrobe looking for something which feels right for the day.

The exercise takes time at first, but once you get used to moving through your own body you will find it can be done in a few minutes. The exercise can benefit everyone, psychic or not.

To add to your well-being for the day, you will find it very beneficial if you now attend to your energy flow.

 Balancing your energy flow

Stand with your feet apart, body straight and hands stretched out above your head. You have now formed two triangles (see diagram). Your arms and hands are in one triangle, the point of which is between your feet. Yours legs and feet are in the other triangle, the point of which is above your head. The triangle formed by your hands brings you refined soul energy to feed your spirit and inner self, and then the energy goes into the earth. The triangle formed by your feet draws up the earth energy which feeds your physical self and then goes into the universe. Your energy is now balanced physically, mentally and spiritually.

Hold the position while you count to ten.

Relax and take five deep breaths. You are now ready to face your day.

During the day, if you experience aches, pains, highs and

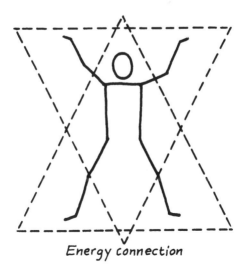

Energy connection

lows in energy or mood, look for a cause. Firstly, is it you? Was it there when you did your exercise that morning? Are you sitting badly? Are you cramped and in need of a stretch? Have you been too intense?

If the problem is your own, deal with the cause and put in your colour. A walk in fresh air can help tremendously. But if you feel the discomfort is not yours, you could be picking up distress signals from someone nearby. To relieve your own distress and help the person concerned, use the following method.

Rescue remedy using colours

If your head is aching, look to see who is holding their head. If your back aches, look to see who is holding their back, and so on.

When you have found the person, you can send healing energy to them. This is done by sensing energy from the middle of your forehead, in the form of a blue light and a green light, needle fine, connecting with the middle of their forehead. Sending the energy takes seconds.

Once you have made the contact, immediately get on with your own activity. Do not hold the contact, do not even think of the person. Sending healing energy takes no time, but will not be received until you stop thinking about it.

The longer you think or concentrate, the longer the person waits to receive help. Thinking and concentration interfere with sending. When the sending is completed, your own discomfort lifts and the person receiving can be relieved of distress.

If the person wishes to remain distressed, they will do so, but you will stop suffering with them. Healing energy does not interfere with the free will of others.

The blue energy transmitted is for physical relief and harmony; the green energy is for inner peace and harmony.

These two colours will relieve distress. This rescue remedy can be used to help crash and accident victims.

Energy shapes for protection

We all need help on occasions when we are in frightening situations, or feel under attack emotionally or physically. Certain energy shapes help when we are ill, distressed or in an environment which is uncomfortable or risky. There are many shapes which can be created in energy around us, but in order for them to work we have to form and energise them. We can also wear the shapes in the form of a pendant. Oval, round, cube and pyramid shapes are all very protective.

Oval shape

To create the oval shape in energy, image yourself surrounded by pink light. Add green and then complete with an outer layer of gold. This is for the days when we feel fragile, vulnerable and unable to face the world but still have to go out. It shields us from noise, bustle, jostling and irritating people. It is ideal for journeys on public transport, visits to crowded supermarkets and places where there is stress. Three colours are used. The inner layer is pink for love and affection. The next layer is green for inner peace. The outer layer is gold for spiritual intunement and courage. The energy will last as long as the need remains, or twelve hours.

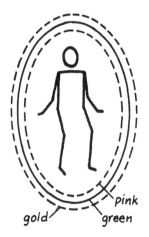

pink

gold   green

Round shape

To create the round shape in energy, image yourself in a bubble of yellow, green and blue light. A round shape is beneficial for those who feel stuck in a situation too small, inadequate or claustrophobic.

Cube shape

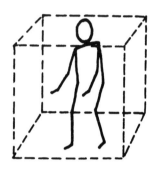

To create the cube shape in energy, visualize four vertical lines as high as yourself, equally spaced around you. Join the tops of the lines to form a square. Join the bottom of the lines to form a square at your feet. A square shape is beneficial for people who are unable to cope with reality and feel insecure. Earthy brown and green are good colour combinations to use for this. The sides of the cube will fill with the colour from the energy lines.

Pyramid shape

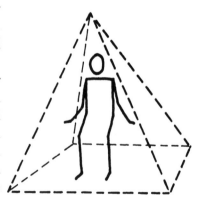

This is a very strong energy shape and has many uses. Different colours can be used depending on the need.

A pink pyramid is useful for relief from deep emotional stress, while a mauve pyramid assists communication. A bright yellow pyramid will relieve fear and paranoia; a blue pyramid will relieve depression.

A green pyramid is used for protection from anger and physical attack. It helps achieve calm after an accident, nightmare or confrontation. It can be placed over a house which is in a high risk area; placed over a car on long, essential journeys; or placed over a car driver who has to drive in bad conditions or in a traumatic state of mind.

The green pyramid can also be used over the bed of a person who is ill in hopital, to prevent them feeling the unease of other patients. In this situation, you add to the green pyramid a colour relevant to the centre in need — light red for heart and arm trouble, mauve for the throat, yellow for stomach and internal organs, green for sexual and leg disorders. The sides of the pyramid will fill with the colour from the energy lines.

To make an energy pyramid, image a spot mid-point above your head. Sense an energy line starting from the mid-point down to the ground, return to the mid-point and visualise another line to the ground until you have four lines, equally spaced around you, from the point to the ground. Join the lines at ground level. Go back to the point and sense the colour shining down and along the lines. Do not fill in the sides — the colour will radiate itself. These shape energies last for twelve hours.

Triangles

If you work in a noisy, unattractive environment with unharmonious people who cause stress you will find it is helpful to place small green triangles around you. If you sit at a desk place a green triangle under the telephone, blotter, work tray or machine. If you live in a flat or house which has disharmony around it, place a green triangle near the doors and windows. This will help prevent unwanted energy entering your space. Cut the triangles from green paper or card. They need only be very small, but each side should be the same length. This energy can prevent disharmony entering into our space.

Achieving calmness

There are many ways to achieve a state of calmness, some of which are described in this chapter.

 ## Breathing exercise

The following exercise should be used for calmness, before or after an interview, audition or confrontation; or before practising in a psychic capacity as a healer/reader.

- Breathe in, counting to three, hold the breath counting to three, breathe out counting to three.
- Breathe in, counting to six, hold the breath counting to six, breathe out counting to six.
- Breathe in, counting to nine, hold the breath counting to nine, breathe out counting to nine.
- Breathe normally.

Exercise to connect with your spirit energy

The next breathing exercise is for use when you are alone or with like-minded friends. It incorporates arm movement and the Om sound. It enables us to contact our inner spirit energy.

Sit quietly and breathe gently, inwardly stating that you wish to contact your spirit energy.

Place both hands in front of your forehead with their backs together, fingers pointing downwards. Breathe in deeply and whilst doing so, lift your hands upwards and outwards, with elbows at shoulder level, your hands either side of your head, palms facing inwards. Breathe out slowly making the Om sound, whilst bringing your hands to rest in front of your throat, with backs together and fingers pointing downwards.

Breathe in deeply and as you do so, lift your hands up past your head and outwards, so that your elbows are level with your shoulders and your palms are facing inwards to face either side of your head. Breathe out making the Om sound whilst bringing your hands to rest in front of your heart, with backs together and fingers pointing downwards.

Breathe in deeply whilst lifting your hands, backs together, and fingers pointing downwards, up past your head and outwards, so that your palms are facing inwards on each side of your head. Breathe out making the Om sound whilst bringing your hands to rest in front of your solar plexus, backs together, fingers pointing downwards.

Breathe in deeply, lifting your hands, backs together and fingers pointing downwards, up past your head and outwards so that your palms are facing inwards on each side of your head.

Breathe out, making the Om sound whilst bringing your hands down to rest on your lap palms downwards.

Sit in that position, allowing the wonderful peace and harmony you have now achieved to flow through you. You are now connected with your spirit energy.

To end the exercise, inwardly state you are disconnecting from the energy, breathe gently. Open your eyes and touch a solid object.

If you wish continue with the next exercise, to connect with your soul energy for balance and intunement, do not disconnect at the end of this exercise but continue as follows.

 Exercise to connect with your soul energy

With your hands palms down on your lap, breathe gently whilst concentrating on your solar plexus and the energy you will be experiencing from the earlier exercise. Sense this energy rising through your body as you breathe gently. This spirit energy is sensed as a white light.

The white light will form a corridor of energy, reaching out to connect with your soul energy. Breathe gently and remain calm and still. When contact with the soul has been made, the white corridor will fill with a stream of colours. A feeling of balance and harmony will be experienced as connection is made with your physical, spirit and soul energies — a state of completeness and calm.

This intunement should not be held for longer than ten minutes when first achieved. If a sense of floating out of the body is experienced, the exercise has been incorrectly carried out and should be ended.

To end the exercise inwardly state you are ready to disconnect. Breathe gently and sense the colours rising, be aware they are doing so. Consciously sense the white beam returning to the solar centre. Touch a solid object and drink some water. Move about the room.

This exercise takes patience. Practise it and gradually build up the connection. If rushed or instant results are expected, it will not succeed.

Focusing

Breathe as shown on page 28 and it will help you prepare for the following exercise. When working with a client it is important for the psychic to focus completely. Outside noises should not be noticed. Personal thoughts should not be paid attention to. A psychic who can only work in a special place or environment is not fully active. You should be able to work anywhere, in any conditions. Here is an exercise to help you learn this essential focusing ability. (This and the following exercise also help concentration in everyday life and are particularly helpful prior to studying.)

 Focusing exercise

Sit in an upright chair facing a lighted candle placed at eye level. Shield the candle from draughts. Set a timer for ten minutes. Inwardly tell yourself you wish to project colour to the candle flame. Sit comfortably, and breathe deeply and slowly to achieve calmness.

Gaze in the direction of the candle and fill your mind with the colour green. Sense the green energy reaching out to the candle and the surrounding area, breathe normally. Practise until you can see the green energy around the candle. Break the connection by looking away from the candle.

Gaze at the candle again. Fill your mind with the colour blue and repeat as above. Look away to disconnect. Try other colours, such as yellow and red and repeat the above exercise.

If, whilst you are concentrating in this way, you begin to think, allow the thoughts to pass by, giving them no attention at all, but steadily holding on to the colour.

If you concentrate on the thought, you will be unable to project the colour and must then stop and attend to the thought to clear it from your mind.

Should this happen, start from the beginning again. By stopping to attend to a thought and having to begin again, you will eventually allow the thoughts to pass by and

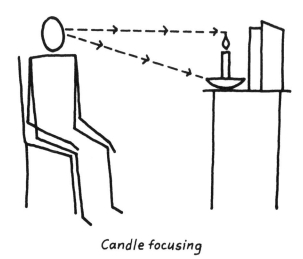

Candle focusing

remain unaffected by them. Even if there is a loud noise, or dozens of people pass through your space, you will still hold the colour and you will have complete focusing control.

When you have achieved this control you can try making the candle flame higher and lower by creating the image in your mind and projecting it to the candle. To end the exercise, extinguish the flame and sip some water. It is possible to see pictures and faces around the candle which should be observed without thought (thinking will activate the imagination and the exercise will be invalidated). The time can be extended when you feel ready.

Once you have gained this control you will be able to concentrate, using your psychic energy, on the person you are working with wherever you are and however noisy it is, remaining totally unconcerned with outside interference or personal thoughts.

Meditation

To help psychics learn discipline and control, a meditative state is also of great assistance. Total intunement with your psychic and inner self will enable you to work with people without your own thoughts and opinions interfering, and you will not be disturbed or put off by external noise. There are many methods of meditation and no perfect way to suit everyone. It is important that each person seeks and finds the way most suitable to their needs.

Purposeful meditation can be used as an exercise in energy control. Any activity which becomes a habit is pointless. It is not only the time spent on meditation which is important but the quality of the content and the purpose behind it. Here is a helpful exercise.

 ### Meditation exercise
Breathe as shown on page 28. Set a buzzer for ten minutes. Sit in a comfortable upright chair. Breathe deeply. Shut your eyes. Image a flower, a tree or a pyramid. Watch the image: it may change. If it does, watch the new image.

If thoughts of everyday matters come into your mind, you should let them pass by. At first you may find the thoughts very persistent and difficult to ignore. If this happens, you should stop and deal with the thought. For instance, a thought that you have not locked the back door can become very persistent; you will need to check the door before you can concentrate on the image. When you have checked, you must start the meditation from the beginning again.

In time you will be at one with the image. Thoughts may float through your consciousness but you will not need to follow them or give them any attention. Background noises and voices will not affect you. You will be totally aware of what you are seeing.

When you are able to watch the image with no interference, it will begin to change, opening up and growing. Pictures will appear in and around it. Observe, but do not think. When you can manage ten minutes in this meditative state, gradually start to extend the time.

When the time allotted for this exercise is over, open your eyes, which will allow the image to fade, and sip some water. This exercise can be carried out daily or when you choose.

PART TWO

The aura

This section is about the aura. I am sure many of you have read or heard about the different colours which can be seen and sensed in the aura. The colours I write about are the ones I 'see'. They may be different from those you are familiar with. I aim here to explain the aura energy, the colours and where they are based. I also give everyday examples in which colour is used to explain a condition or emotion.

I have spent a great many years studying the aura and hope the following results of that study and practice will clarify and give you information and, perhaps, a new way of understanding what an aura is.

# The aura

We register energy through all our senses. The energy of the aura is sensed in colour. It can also be sensed by holding our hands near the body.

The aura is energy which permeates and surrounds each of us. It is sensed as layers of colour which vibrate and radiate. The electro-magnetic glow which is the second of these layers, and is seen as a white light, can also be seen around rocks, plants and stones. The aura energy holds a record of all that has happened to and around the object, be it animate or inanimate. Where there is a spirit present, as with living humans and creatures, the spirit energy combines with physical energy and concentrates in various parts of the body. These concentrated energy centres are sometimes called 'chakras' which means 'wheel' in Sanskrit. For clarity I call them the 'inner centres' as they are based in, and shine through, the physical body.

The easiest energies for psychics to tune into are the inner centre colours which shine through the electro-magnetic layer. These are blue, mauve, pink/red, yellow, green and blue/green. They show spirit energy, health and balance and are based at the centre of living creatures. These inner centre colours are the same for all living beings (see page 44).

Close to the body is the electro-magnetic layer which is clear and glows strongly. Although this is the second layer, it can appear to some to be the first. Some psychics see this layer tinged with colour. This is a reflection of the colours from the inner centres and surrounding energy. This electro-magnetic layer is the physical energy field and is magnetic. When a person is unbalanced, fatigued or distressed in any way, this layer is affected. The strong uniform glow, which is normally about half an inch deep around the body, will appear agitated near the area in distress. When a person is excited for any reason, the whole of this layer glows very brightly all around the body. If they are thinking, it is easier to see around the head. The inner centre colours can be seen around this energy.

Around these two aura layers the outer aura colours can be sensed. These layers record information relative to past and present growth, experience, potential, strengths and weaknesses — in fact all that has occurred in the present life. Also recorded in colour are links to the soul, past life experiences, images, knowledge and wisdom. The aura is a complete record of the total spiritual and physical being. These colours vary from person to person, and each colour has many meanings depending on where it is located and on its exact shade.

Some auras are very wide, others are not. It is the quality of the colours, the peace, the energy and the overall sense of awareness, responsibility and dignity which matter, not how large the aura happens to be.

A psychic tunes into the aura record of a person and senses the energy received as pictures, thoughts, feelings and/or words. Some psychics can link into the aura for past life information. Very few can see the entire aura around a person. Some can sense the colours but not see them.

When tuning into a person to help them with healing energy, it is usually the inner centre colours which will be seen or sensed first. If the inner centre colours are seen or sensed, they give clues as to the cause of illness and imbalance. For example, if a yellow glow or flash of yellow is sensed near the throat area of a person complaining of laryngitis, this means the trouble is caused by fear. If red is observed near the solar/courage centre, the person will be experiencing stomach or digestive troubles. The red signifies that anger is causing the imbalance and fear. When a depressed person has pink near the top of their head, it means that the depression is caused through lack of love and understanding. Healing energy can then be given, and the cause found, to help the person to help him or herself.

To sharpen the psychic ability to see the aura it is advisable to start by tuning into the electro-magnetic layer, which is next to the body and easiest to sense. This is the second aura layer. It is seen as a white glow around the entire body.

Tuning into the electro-magnetic layer

Inwardly tell yourself you wish to see the aura. Face the person. Breathe gently and clear the mind. Look through or off centre, not at the person. The aura cannot be sensed by staring with the physical eyes.

Defocus and gaze around the head and shoulder area. It takes practice, but the glow can be seen if the eyes are defocused.

Make sure the aura is being observed and not an optical illusion. When the glow can be seen, keep the eyes unfocused and look away from the person. If the glow is still visible it is optical and not valid. If the glow remains around the person it is the aura.

Practise when sitting with friends. Look at each person in turn. The more you practise, the easier it becomes.

When this layer can be seen, it is easier to see the colours surrounding it. The colours are moving, fluctuating, deepening and fading all the time. They are not solid but are similar to the colours reflected when sunlight shines through stained glass.

Defocus and gently look in the area surrounding the person. The colours are usually easier to see around the head and shoulders. It is not easy to hold on to the colours, as they constantly move. A flash or a momentary glow of colour is normally all that is seen.

The outer aura field is like fingerprints, in that no two people can have the same patterns.

It is very unwise purposefully to move and pull at the aura energies of another person, especially if the psychic cannot see the aura clearly or feel it accurately. This practice can change the balance of a person. The aura can balance itself if healing energy is given and the cause of the imbalance is found and corrected.

Auras do not have holes in them, disappear or leak. They can release energy, but this energy comes from the electro-magnetic layer nearest the body. The aura in its entirety is self-contained.

A healer transfers energy to those in need. Some healers cannot see or sense the energy colours and so doubt their ability to heal. If a healer cannot 'see' the colour vibrations, it does not affect the energy flow in any way. The healing energy will always adjust to suit the patient, irrespective of the healer's ability.

You could try developing your colour sensitivity by looking at a coloured card and then observing a person. Stare for several minutes at a card coloured mid-blue until the colour can be seen when your eyes are closed. Now quickly open your eyes and observe the person's upper head. The blue will optically be impressed around it. The brain will accept the colour through the eyes and the psychic will find that the aura blue of the area can eventually be seen without using the card first. Then try the other centre colours.

Some healers used coloured light on their patient — either coloured bulbs or light shining through stained glass. This can activate the healer's ability to see the aura colour as well as helping the patient.

ⵝ *Aura clearing*

All people can release into the atmosphere the energy from the electro-magnetic energy which surrounds us. When this release is negative it can adversely affect the well-being of others; when it is positive it can create a feeling of joy and peace.

If we are energised and reasonably active, we will repel unwanted energies naturally. When we shake or tremble without any obvious reason, it is usually the aura shaking off unwanted energy. However if our energy is low or we are unwell, depressed, angry, or in negative company too long, it is possible for this energy to attach to us, build up and gradually be absorbed through our aura. It can form patches of dull or agitated energy around us.

Some people feel these negative areas as a numbness or a pressure, and think it is a spirit entity. Psychics can sense these areas on people and mistakenly confirm them as entities, or even tell the person they are possessed. This is not so, and causes a great deal of unnecessary fear and distress to the person concerned.

Negative energy which has not cleared naturally can and should be cleared from the aura by a psychic healer. Aura clearing, as with healing, can be done by energy alone, but most people like to see or feel things happening physically.

 ## Exercise to clear the aura

The person to be cleared should stand with feet apart, arms loosely at the sides. As the negativity will be concentrated on the electro-magnetic layer next to the body, the psychic does not need to touch the person and works about two inches away from their skin surface. The healer should inwardly tell him or herself that they wish to clear the aura.

Begin above their head, keep your thumbs together, and

spread out your hands. Move your hands down the person, not touching them, until you reach the floor. Go back above the head again and, moving round the person in a clockwise direction, brush from above the head to the floor until you have encircled them. Do sides, arms, inner legs and finally under each foot. The cleared person should then shake their body, including their feet.

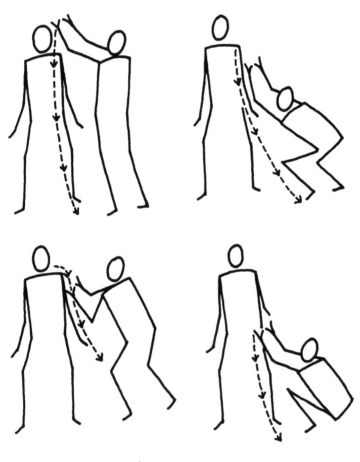

Aura clearing

This aura clearing exercise can be repeated if necessary. The person being treated should feel cool or glowing when the aura has been properly cleared and cleaned.

 ## Clearing your own aura

Inwardly tell yourself that you wish to clear your own aura. Breathe deeply and as you breathe out sense a circle of energy above your head as wide as yourself. Sense the energy turning clockwise as it moves down your body. This will remove negative energy from your own aura field. The energy will go down into the earth where the energy will neutralise. This method can also be used on other people, by projecting the ring of energy you have made to them. To do this, project the circle of energy you have sensed to the person who needs help by imaging the ring of energy around their upper head. It will clear their aura and neutralise unwanted energy.

The aura can become agitated when we are near a person who is incompatible and can cause us to feel uncomfortable in their company. Let's take an example. When we see someone who attracts us we may ask friends about the person, and they could assure us that the person is very good company, friendly and worth meeting; but as soon as we stand near that person we know we do not like them at all. We feel ill at ease and even afraid. This is because however physically attractive a person appears, their aura tells the truth about them. A sensitive person will sense that all is not as it seems on the surface.

We should never disregard this sense, as it will save us a great deal of trouble if we pay heed to it. The aura has registered that the person is not compatible and it would be wise to retreat. If you should meet them again, stand near them and take note of how you feel. It may only have been a temporary incompatibility, but if the unease repeats itself, you would be wise not to get too friendly.

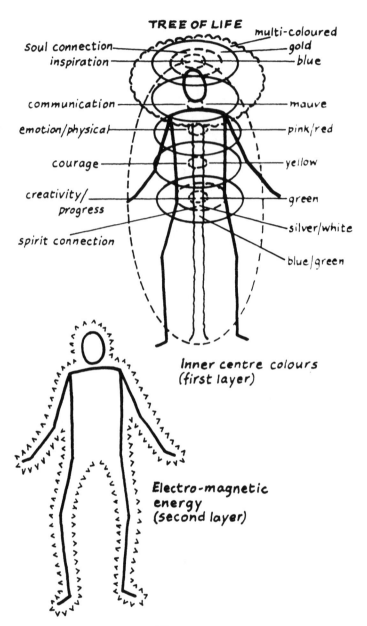

TREE OF LIFE

Soul connection — multi-coloured
inspiration — gold
— blue

communication — mauve

emotion/physical — pink/red

courage — yellow

creativity/progress — green

spirit connection — silver/white

— blue/green

Inner centre colours
(first layer)

Electro-magnetic
energy
(second layer)

The aura

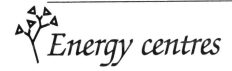

Energy centres

Colour and connection

We all have energy centres (sometimes called chakras) and these are based on the tree of life centre which flows through the core of our physical body. Each pulsates in its own space and links into all other centres.

When healing energy is transferred to a person in need, it will help them to balance and harmonise these centres. When we are out of balance, all the centres are affected to a greater or lesser degree and as the healer works down the body each centre is energised.

Inspiration and motivation – blue

Location: The upper head to the end of the nose.

This energy affects the upper head, eyes and nose, and is deep blue. It is centred at the top of the head. It glows deeply blue when the person is in tune with their inner self, connected with inspired thought or spiritual intunement.

When this centre is under-energised or imbalanced, the blue can become so dark that it feels like a black cloud and interferes with positive action or thought; or the blue energy can become pale and thin, seeping into the aura field and tingeing it all with blue. This causes depression and affects all the centres.

This blue energy can be felt, and the person will say they 'feel blue' or they 'have the blues'. A certain type of sad, soulful music is known as the blues.

Energy imbalance in this centre causes lethargy, depression, suicidal thought, sadness, loneliness and an overall feeling of hopelessness. Physically it causes headache and general body pains. When working on this centre, blue energy should be transferred to the person. If imbalance and depression have been sensed, proceed as follows.

Dealing with imbalance

Place one of your hands on the top of their head and sense blue energy entering. Place your other hand on the cause centre. (If the depression is found to be caused by emotional upsets, your other hand should be placed on the emotion centre, for example. If the cause is found to be fear, your other hand should be placed on the courage centre.) Sense or see the relevant colours entering the centres concerned. Energise with blue and move to the next centre.

Communication – mauve

Location: The lower head from the end of the nose, including the ears, jaw, back and front neck, to the collar bone.

This is a mauve energy and in its balanced, harmonised state encourages communication with our fellow humans, animals, nature and self. It is the energy behind our words. It enables us to convey our thoughts, hopes and dreams to others, which in turn can inspire them to greater things. When communication energy is translated into sound it can have a profound positive or negative affect on those who hear, and on the atmosphere of the planet. For that reason, all the sounds that we make should be carefully vetted for tone as well as content. Whichever way we communicate, the energy comes from this centre.

A person who communicates on a very fine, deep spiritual note will have deep violet near this centre. The centre will become imbalanced if the person is ignoring physical reality and communication and causing stress through neglect of their mind and body. When communication becomes difficult or impossible, the mauve energy becomes disturbed. If the person is frustrated, intense or talks continuously, is afraid to speak or does not want to speak, the mauve will change to intense or pale shades. The person may attract a sore throat, painful neck glands, constriction, or neck and shoulder pains.

The healer will try to ascertain the cause of the imbalance and help the person to correct it. Energise with mauve.

Emotions/physical energy – pink and red

Location: Upper body from the collar bone to the mid-rib area including shoulders, arms, hands, heart and lungs.

This centre is sensed as a pink energy interlaced with red, centred in the heart area. The pink represents the emotions and the red the physical. These colours work individually and together.

When a person is emotionally balanced and physically healthy the pink and red are seen in harmony together, gently pulsating. The person will feel happy and energised. If a person is unhappy through lack of love and care, the pink energy can become pale and de-energised. It can affect the arms, causing them to feel weak or painful. It can also affect the heart, causing it to ache, and a general lethargy can result.

Resentment, anger and rejection can cause the deep pink emotion energy to become intense and deeply coloured. It then links into the red physical energy and can result in violent behaviour. This can create pain in the heart area and loss of breath. By linking into all the other centres it produces a person who is incoherent, self-destructive, violent and totally unreasonable.

When the physical is unbalanced, the red energy can become very pale and link into the pink, causing a lack of interest in partners and/or a feeling of rejection which can give rise to cold anger and irrational behaviour.

If the person becomes angry, the red energy begins to build up near the heart until it cannot be contained and explodes in temper. This happens very quickly in some people and they are soon in balance again. Others take longer to build up and longer to recover.

The more intense the energy, the easier it is to see. In fact some people sense their own red energy rising and say: 'I saw red!' Their face will also become red as the physical energy is released. When we are in love we have a rosy glow around the upper body.

The healer transfers pink energy interlaced by red into the centre, working across the upper body.

Courage – golden yellow

Location: Centre of the body, from mid-rib to the top of the hips.

This energy is a deep golden yellow which, in its balanced, harmonious state, gives rise to courage, determination, selfless action and steadfastness.

The centre glows like the sun and is known as the solar centre. This energy band physically affects the stomach, liver, kidneys, digestion and intestines. In its negative state it can cause loss of appetite, nausea, stomach cramps, fluttering sensations in the stomach, diarrhoea and loss of bladder control. It can also affect the back muscles, causing pain. The imbalanced yellow energy affects other centres: it can cause heart palpitations, loss of memory, inability to speak and even paralysis of the arms and legs. The trigger of this negative chain is fear.

The healer will seek the cause of the fear and this will alleviate some of the symptoms. The centre attracts and absorbs atmosphere. If a person is secure and balanced any negativity will be repelled, but those who are in a low energy state will attract and absorb the energy around them, gradually mirroring the people they spend time with. A low-energy person can help themselves by finding positive, energised people and atmospheres.

The healer transfers deep golden yellow to this centre to build up its positive aspects and help overcome fear.

There is a mid-band of energy between emotion and

courage which, when balanced, is an apricot colour. This is an overlap of deep pink and yellow. If anger in the emotion centre causes red to be predominant and yellow is released from the solar centre through fear, the overlap becomes orange. When this band is full of orange energy it causes violence and unthinking destruction. If a person has this overlap of orange, until the cause of the fear-related anger is found they are advised not to eat or drink anything from the orange fruit or to eat food coloured orange. They should also avoid wearing orange and looking at the colour. Many children who are labelled hyper-active or destructive can be calmed by removing orange from their diet and sight.

Creativity and progress — green
Location: From the top of the hips to beneath the feet.

This energy physically affects the reproductive organs, the legs and the feet, and is coloured green. When it is used in creative activity, the person will feel happy, balanced and productive.

Should sexual activity not occur or be rare, either by choice or lack of opportunity, the person can become tense and de-energised. The tension can be relieved by increasing involvement in creative activities to utilise the energy and to help others to progress.

Being envious of other people's achievements causes green to be released and gives rise to the saying: 'Green with envy'. If the energy is not used sexually or creatively, the person can experience constipation, swellings, and pain in the groin and lower back. If a person is unable to progress physically or spiritually, whether by choice, circumstances or fear, the energy can cause their legs and feet to become painful.

A woman who desperately wants a child can concentrate the creative energy so intensely that it becomes counter-productive, affecting the natural body cycle. It helps some women if they hold a new-born child on their lap. The creative energy can become stronger, thereby relaxing the physical system.

When there is imbalance in the creative centre, all centres are affected; depression, and loss of confidence and self-respect, can occur. The person can experience a tingling or burning sensation in their hands and feet, lower back pains and general debility.

Transfer green energy.

Nerve centre — deep green/blue

Location: Spine.

This energy works through the nervous system and flows through every nerve in the body. It is a deep green/blue.

Should a centre be unbalanced, the nervous energy in that centre will be alerted. If the imbalance is serious, a chain reaction can occur which will cause all the centres, whether involved in the crisis or not, to malfunction. The malfunction can cause a breakdown in communication and eventually the whole system, physical and spiritual, becomes imbalanced and seems to be non-functioning.

If a person seeks help early in the crisis, the sense of shutdown can be averted. The centres affected can be balanced with their relevant energy colours, and the nerve centre calmed and soothed with deep green/blue energy.

Spirit energy centre — silver/white (also called Kundalini)

Location: Base of spine, between the creative and nervous energy centres.

This centre is the source of energy for the spirit. Should a person be afraid of this energy centre or ignore their spirit/soul needs, it will become low in energy and imbalanced. The person will be using energy from the other centres, denying the flow to replenish the spirit. This can eventually reach a stage where the physical well-being is affected, which in turn can lead to robotic behaviour. Some people seek help in this crisis and see it as a sign to change their ways.

A healer will fill the person with silver-white energy if he or she senses this crisis in its early stages. This energy can help balance the physical and the spiritual life, to allow change to be made naturally.

PART THREE

Healers and healing energy

This section explains healers and the energy they transmit to other people. It includes some reasons for illness and imbalance, how to sense and balance the inner centres, and the value of colour, stones and quartz in healing sessions.

Various methods of transmitting healing energy are shown. The needs and beliefs of each person are different and a psychic will endeavour to accommodate these when working in a healing capacity. Some people need to feel the hands of the healer whilst being treated, some do not.

Healers and healing energy

A person who is psychic transfers healing energy to those in need. All living things have a natural self-healing ability, but on occasions this ability is unable to function due to low energy. No one can cure another person; a psychic can give the healing energy, but the receiver's own centres distribute it where it is most required.

Healing energy is given primarily to balance and encourage the positive aspects and energies of a person. It is essential to work on the whole person, not one part.

Energy becomes imbalanced where there is a malfunction, whether it be a broken bone, a diseased organ, pollution or unhappiness. Attitude is very important. Acceptance of an imbalance can make it seem natural, and people then begin to live with it instead of seeking its cause.

When a healer is near a person in need, the healing energy will automatically begin to flow. It will clear and energise the healer first, and then move to the person in need. It will go where it is most needed by the patient to correct imbalance, to energise and to enable the natural self-healing ability to activate as soon as possible.

All psychics transfer healing energy, even those who are unaware they have the ability or appear to have no other psychic talent. Healing energy can be transferred by words or sounds, even via a telephone, or by touch. It can also be transmitted to people near or far away.

Many healers use their hands, either on or near the person in need. Touch is psychologically beneficial, but not necessary to transfer healing energy. Touch shows care, and many people de-energise because no one cares enough to touch them lovingly and boost their self-healing properties. Many healers feel they are in greater contact if they use touch. It is best to adapt to suit the need of the person.

If a person's skin is too sore to touch, moving the hands

above the skin works just as well. In some cases a person needs healing but declines to be touched. They may have a conflict between their religious beliefs and their desperate need to feel well. By avoiding touch they are able to appease their conscience and benefit from the healing energy. Some prefer the healer to work near the body but not on it. Some healers prefer to energise via the aura and not to touch the physical body. When working, the healer should keep his or her personal religious, political and sexual preferences totally private. Give help to anyone in need.

The healing techniques explained in this book are based on the belief that it is important to find the cause of the trouble or pain and to work on that cause. It is possible, of course, to remove pain, but if the reason behind it has not been found then the pain will return. A pain is an alarm signal: it is foolish to switch off an alarm without finding why it has been activated.

If the person does not wish to get well, they will not. Psychic reading can then be used to find out why they want to hold on to the pain and discomfort. This can help the person to be more positive, using the healing energy to deal with the fear or inability to cope which is causing their distress.

If you do not practise cause-finding, it does not mean that you will be less able to transfer the healing energy to the person in need. The person can seek the cause within himself or herself, or seek assistance elsewhere. The healing energy will complement other treatments.

Laughter is very important in healing work. If the person being treated is tight-lipped and/or nervous, a smile helps them to relax and absorb the healing energy offered.

People can believe they are healers because they work in a healing group which achieves good results. But only psychics can transfer the healing energy to others; and in a group which has a psychic present, healing will be transferred by the psychic to all present. If people have their hands on a person it will seem they are transferring their healing energy to the patient. The idea that everyone can heal others has caused confusion and disappointment. People without the ability find they can only function with certain companions, and not on their own.

All people in caring professions become disillusioned at times, wondering if they are doing any good at all, even dreading at times the steady flow of imbalanced people seeking help. Healers are no different. It is natural to question, but most people find this phase passes.

A healer and patient should not feel disappointed after a healing session if an imbalance remains. It could be a choice, or perhaps the reasons for it have not been found. Causes should be sought and, if possible, alternative approaches to life found.

Some people manifest an illness because they need a reason to prevent them doing something. A minor disability, such as a headache or cold, can get a day or two off from work which is boring, which they resent, or which they are afraid of. By the time they return, someone else has attended to the problem. They do not feel guilty — they believe they really did have a headache or a cold. The energy of the thought behind a pretended illness can, on occasion, manifest and the pretence becomes a reality.

A person who finds it hard to communicate either through embarrassment or through fear can develop a series of throat infections, sometimes so severe that they are advised not to speak for a week or months.

The energy of fear can cause upset in the stomach, bowels, bladder or digestion. These upsets can and will recur until the fear is faced or removed. Fear can also cause heart palpitations. Fear of, or through, humiliation can cause a complete breakdown of the physical structure,

· resulting in paralysis. Fear of promotion or progress can cause loss of use in the legs. Fear of sex or distaste of a partner can cause rashes to occur in the genital area.

The energy of pent-up resentment can cause heart pain, blood pressure, severe headaches and stomach cramps. Suppression of feelings, whether through fear or inhibition, can affect not only the physical organs but the delicate balance of nervous energy as well. Nervous tension or repression can manifest in skin disorders, speech abnormalities and painful joints. A person who refuses to face a situation can develop a facial rash; one who does not want to see what is happening around them can develop eye troubles to cloud their vision. A person who is afraid to hear the truth about him or herself, or a situation, can develop deafness to dull his or her hearing.

Some people who feel alone, unnoticed or uninteresting can unknowingly cause quite major symptoms to appear which attract the maximum of attention. They do not always want to be healed, as they like the attention they get. They become professionally ill. Others unknowingly make themselves unattractive through weight loss or gain when needing an excuse to end a relationship. Weight loss or gain can also occur when a person is lonely and cannot attract a partner or friends. They feel their lack of attraction is due to their size, and do not look for other causes.

Lack of love and understanding can cause weak heart symptoms, or the loss of use of arms or hands. Loneliness can cause vagueness, a loss of reality. An unhealthy or unsympathetic environment at home or work can result in loss of energy, lethargy, depression and short temper. Lack of fresh air and incorrect breathing aggravates all illness and disease.

All these causes can result in very genuine physical symptoms and pain. Once the reason behind the symptom and pain has been established, faced, removed or understood, the person can reach a balanced, healthy state of being.

But not all illness or unease is caused by the person's defence system over-reacting and malfunctioning. Many people become ill from stress, pollution, drug and alcohol abuse or unsuitable diet. Accidents can occur through inattention. People can be attacked, terrorised. The causes of these imbalances are findable, and appropriate counselling can be found to give ongoing help and care. Healing energy complements all treatments.

Arguments and quarrels use energy and can cause nervous and mental debility. Altercations can be habit-forming, becoming so normal that they lose their impact whilst gradually undermining a relationship until it is beyond repair. During an argument, the exchange of words may reach the lowest ebb. Hurtful words are exchanged, none of which can be erased afterwards however much they are regretted, leaving energy patterns on the mind and the atmosphere.

If you as the healer can sense or see the aura centre colours, you will have a valuable clue as to the cause of imbalance. Yellow, for instance, near the neck area, means there is trouble communicating, because of fear. A person who has green at the top of the head is depressed because of a lack of creativity and progress. A person who has yellow near their legs will have trouble walking due to fear.

A patient's first appointment is their first step towards well-being. Each meeting is a step forward towards their own self-reliance and good health potential. If a person continues to need a healer for the same reasons without any apparent improvement, either the healer is not working well with that person or the person has become dependent on the healer. Assessment of the situation should be made regularly.

After the twenty to thirty minutes' healing energy

treatment has been completed, the patient should be given an appointment for one week hence. You should not hold thoughts of the patient after they leave. Healing energy only reaches the person in need after thinking about them has ceased. After four consecutive meetings, assess their progress. The time between appointments should be lengthened gradually until the person is well and in control.

Touch healing

There is no one way of healing which suits, or works for, everyone. Each person should find the method which suits them. Those who come to healers have either found that our way suits them, that it complements other treatment they are having, or have tried every other way and have turned to us in despair.

The following method uses touch and colour. We do not energise a part of a person, we energise the complete person. By using a basic pattern, you will be able to forget your hands, sense the colours and temperature changes, and pick up helpful information on the cause of the pain or problem.

The patient can stand, lie down or sit, but you may prefer him or her to sit on a stool or straight-backed chair, using a low stool yourself to sit on when attending to the legs and feet.

The touch healing sequence

Sit the patient slightly forward on the chair so that you can get your hand between them and the chair back. It helps if they remove their shoes and spectacles, if worn. There is no need for them to remove any article of clothing as the healing energy will go through anything. The shoes are removed to make it easier for you to touch the feet; also to let the feet cool and make handling more pleasant. Make sure the patient's feet can touch the ground.

The hands of the patient should be placed palms down on their thighs, with their feet slightly apart on the floor. Check their back is straight. Begin by holding their hands and welcoming them. This initial hand contact is for you to connect. You may feel their pain or sense their problem. Ask them to tell you their reason for coming. This opens up communication and energy flow. Replace their hands and stand behind them, placing your hands on their shoulders. Use both hands at all times. Breathe quietly for a few seconds and begin, using blue energy.

1 Put your two index fingers on the bridge of their nose. Keeping your fingers together, lightly bring them up the forehead, over the top and down the back of their head, the back of their neck and off at the shoulders. Do this three or more times, each time more slowly.

2 Now place your thumbs on the bridge of their nose and, keeping them together, lightly bring them up the forehead. As you come over the head allow your hands to fan out over the sides of the head. Bring the thumbs together down the back of the head and neck and off at the shoulders. Do this three times or more, each time more slowly.

Do not manipulate, rub in or use pressure with this healing method, and take your hands off at the nearest exit — in this case the shoulders. Point your hands downwards towards the floor to remove unwanted energy.

The exercise so far is for soothing confusion, fear and tension. First you dealt with the confusion, then you brought in harmony.

3 Put your finger-tips at the centre of the forehead and

stroke outward over the temples and off at the ears. Do this three times, each time more slowly, to remove stress.

4 Place your finger-tips at the top of their nose and lightly stroke upwards past the hairline. Do this three times or more, to lift the energy.

5 Place your fingers together on their forehead and bring your hands down, pausing over the eyes; using one finger on each hand, gently move outward under the eyes, then off at the ears. Repeat. The reason for going down to the eyes is to give the patient a chance to close them. If you bring your hands up to the eyes there is a danger of putting your finger in them, which is inclined to shatter the peaceful harmony you are trying to achieve!

6 Gently stroke down the nose with your fingers. This helps air flow.

7 Using mauve energy, cup the jaw with one hand on each side of the face, then pause. This is for communication.

8 Gently lift your hands to cover their ears, and pause. Then go over the top of the ears, down the back of the ears, down the sides of the neck and off at the shoulder exit. Repeat.

9 Cup your hands round the front of the neck. Do not use any pressure here, or the person will begin to choke and harmony will be lost!

10 The nape of the neck is next. Putting your thumbs at the bottom of the skull, stroke downward to the base of the neck vertebra and off at the shoulders. Repeat three or more times.

11 Place one hand each side of the neck vertebra and gently stroke down and off at the shoulders. This clears negative energy build-up.

12 Using green/blue energy stand to one side of the patient, place one hand on the breast bone and, with the other, brush down from top to botttom of the spine, using long, slow movements, three or four times. Now brush each side of the spine until all the back has been brushed top to bottom. This soothes and calms the nervous system.

13 With pink/red energy put one hand in front of the shoulder and the other at the back, making a sandwich. Pause. Lift your hands and work horizontally across the body. Repeat this until you reach the other shoulder. Move your hands down and continue to work across the body a band at a time. Change to yellow energy at mid-rib, and work across this band to the hip joints. Go back, put one hand on the solar plexus and the other in the small of the back, and pause. This is a vital energy centre which, when de-energised, can cause backache. Work across the hip band in green for creative energy.

14 Sit on your low stool in front of the patient. Gently lift one of their hands and place it over the other. Put one of your hands behind their hip and the other on their thigh. Move both hands downward in one long movement and bring your hands off at the toes. Put your hands on the thigh and work down to the knee. Pause at the knee joint, then work down to the ankle.

Place the foot on your lap and, with both hands, make a backward circular movement behind the ankle bone, then round the ankle bone. Stroke the foot from ankle to toes. Gently spread the ball of the foot and stroke each toe individually from base to tip. Place the foot between your hands and pause. Put the foot back on the floor, transfer their hands to the finished leg and repeat the exercise on the other leg. When both legs and feet are completed, put their hands back on each leg.

15 Using pink/red energy, stand by one shoulder and hold the shoulder joint between your hands. Move your hands down the arm, the hand, and off at the fingers in one movement. Return to the shoulder and work down from shoulder to elbow. Pause at the elbow, then work from the elbow to the wrist and pause at this joint. Take their hand and spread it out gently. Stroke each finger from the base and off at the finger tip. Put their hand between both of your own and pause. Replace their hand on the leg. Repeat the exercise with the other arm and hand.

If your hands move or pause, do not interfere. If they go to an area other than the one you have reached, allow them to do so.

16 Return to any spot which you felt was distressed, either because the patient said so or because you felt it yourself.

17 Stand behind the person and place your hands on their shoulders, resting their head against you to give comfort and compassion.

18 Stand in front of the person and put both their hands together, enclosed in your own; hold them for a few seconds. You are encircling them with energy by this action and making sure they retain the energy you have transferred to them. Thank them for coming. Place their hands back on their legs and move away. Do not hover over the patient when you have finished, because they need to adjust and clear their space. The energy given becomes theirs. Ask them to stand and stretch into their own space when they feel ready to do so.

19 Your final action when the person has left, and before touching another person, is to brush your hands together to signify the finish. This ensures you do not carry the patient's energies on you or on to the next person.

20 Wash your hands.

Avoid walking in front of the patient during the session.

If you prefer your patient to lie on a couch, use the same healing method but work on the front of the body, then the back. Sit them up to do the head and neck, and finish by placing their hands together.

When you have established this basic method of healing, your hands will work by themselves, leaving you free to sense and feel the cause of the imbalance.

Always work downward. Humans, like animals, become irritated and ill-at-ease if stroked the wrong way. We are most comfortable when stroked downward. The saying 'Someone has rubbed you up the wrong way,' comes from this fact.

If for any reason you are unable to use this method of healing, people will be greatly comforted if you can hold their hands and their feet and stroke their forehead, transferring the healing colours as you do so.

As your hands are working down the body, you may sense and record temperature changes; hot or cold, or a vibration, recorded as a tingling or quivering in the hands. Some healers feel one or all of these. It is a sign of their own energy flowing to the patient, or the energy of the patient showing balance and imbalance.

Other healers cannot feel anything at all, but their patient can feel the energy flowing to them. It really does not matter who feels what. It is not a sign that one healer is better than another.

If the healer does not experience the above signs, they are still transferring healing energy and should not be concerned about what they cannot feel or see.

A person does not become ill or feel pain or discomfort from a session with a healer. If the healer is lacking in compassion and is seeing people for personal ego or financial reasons only, they can still help. But obviously the energy given will be low in care and understanding and the patient will not benefit very much from the session.

If a healer is working well, is tuned into the energy and keeps detached, he or she will not become tired. In fact, he or she will become energised. A psychic who complains of being 'drained' after working is not tuned into the energy correctly and can be giving his or her own energy reserves to others. These people should check they know what they are doing and learn to tune in properly: if they cannot, it may be a sign that they are not natural healers.

Laser healing

Some psychics have the ability to concentrate their energy into fine, intense beams of light which can be directed to the person in need. This method of transferring the healing energy is intensive and used for short periods only. It is called laser healing.

Laser healing sequence

Sit with the patient opposite you, either sitting or lying down. Make contact by holding their hand for a few seconds to tune into their problem and ascertain which energy centre the problem is centred in.

From your mid-forehead send one needle-fine blue light and one green light to their mid-forehead. Hold the two colours in that position until contact is made, which is felt by the psychic and/or the person as a warm/cold/tingling feeling on the forehead area. This takes approximately ten seconds.

When this contact has been established, add to the

green and blue a needle-fine laser beam in the colour of the centre affected. For example, if the problem is depression, blue is added; if it is communication, mauve is added; if it is emotional, add deep pink; fear requires yellow; creativity needs green.

When this colour has been added, move the three colours down from the forehead to the centre in question. Hold all three at a specific point in the centre if known, then spread them out over the area for approximately ten seconds.

Take the three colours to a point approximately twelve inches about their head, then add as many colours as you can to form an arc as wide as the person. Sweep this arc of coloured light beams down the person to below their feet. Switch the colours out by sensing them fading away.

Sit quietly for a minute or two, not touching the person. Then put their hands together to circulate the energies. Move away from the person and brush your hands to clear the contact.

This method can be used to complement touch healing or as a separate healing technique. It activates energy and revitalises.

Absent healing

When a person is unable to visit a healer, healing energy can be transmitted to them. The healer and patient do not need to know each other, the healing energy will still be received. Some people prefer to think of the healer at a pre-arranged time and link by thinking of colours and images. They are showing a willingness to get well. A progress report should be sent to the healer, as this keeps a contact between the healer and the patient.

Choose a time which you can set aside for the work. Tell your patients what time this is so they can participate if they wish.

The healing energy can be sent to, and received in, any part of the world. The energy reaches the patient the moment the healer releases it. Thinking delays the release of energy.

You can use photographs in absent healing as a reference point. If you do not have a photograph to work from, have the person's name on a piece of paper.

The absent healing sequence

Sit quietly at the chosen time with your photographs and names face down in front of you. Breathe deeply. Look at the first picture or name, then look in front of you and image an upright human shape.

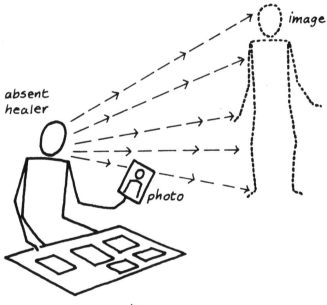

image

absent healer

photo

Absent healing

It is not necessary to have any features as long as it is a complete, upright shape. If the patient has no legs or arms, or is unable to stand, you still image them as a complete figure.

Send colour energy. If the person is imbalanced in the solar centre, for example, send yellow. Then cover the image with all colours, as a rainbow or wash. If they are unwell in the emotional centre, send pink. Send yellow for courage, or green for creativity. If the cause of the illness is unknown, send green and blue first and then all colours. If you are unable to sense colours, send white light to cover the image. Some healers who cannot sense or image colours find it helpful if they look at coloured cards or coloured glass when doing this work.

Turn the photograph or sheet of paper over and repeat with the next one until all the photographs and names have been dealt with. Put them away until the same time next day.

Absent healing, as with any healing, is totally harmless. It cannot heal a person who chooses to remain unwell, whatever their reasons!

The energy will assist the person to become strong and positive, if that is their need, or can give them peace of mind, strength of purpose, will to live, or alleviation of pain or depression. If they choose to remain imbalanced and ill, they have a reason, and until they choose to deal with the cause they will not change. In helping an imbalanced person think more clearly, and feel stronger in purpose, the energy assists them to want to help themselves.

If, on occasions, you send the energy at a different time from your set time, it will still be received. If you are unable to send it, or forget, the healing energy will automatically transmit for one or two days.

If you are away from home, at a social function, even at

the theatre or cinema at the usual time of your sending, go through the names in your mind. Let them run through above thought. The energy will still reach the recipient.

 ## Health update by psychic means

If you do not receive a report on your patient, use a photograph or their name to tune into them and receive an update on their health. A psychic can tune into the person pictured in a photograph and sense how they are. Not all psychics will be able to do this, but it is very helpful in absent healing. Have a pad and pencil handy to record what you sense. Sit comfortably and take a few slow breaths. Hold the photograph in your fingers. Do not think – sense.

The photograph will move around in your fingers. Feel the surface and register any roughness, smoothness or marks which stand out. Also note your own physical sensations and feelings. All you feel gives an indication of the condition of the person in the photograph. It is wise not to gaze at the person in the picture as you can get a false impression. The picture may be very old and the person very changed.

As well as sending absent healing individually, healers can combine their energies to send to people, countries and deprived areas and to boost their personal energy and needs.

 ## The group absent healing sequence

The healers should be in harmony with each other and sit in a circle, which enables the energy to build up in the centre. One member should be designated the leader of the group and the person on his or her left hand should recite the names of all those people they know are in need. They can then add a country which they feel needs help and end by saying: 'and myself'. Energy rings of colour will form a spiral in front of them, which will include them when they say 'and myself'. The next person on the left then lists names, a country and ends with: 'and myself'. They then form their spirals of moving colour, while the next person continues, and so on around the circle until it is the turn of the leader.

The leader says names, a country, absent members of the group, including any project or special need not covered by the others, and ends 'and myself'.

The healing energy will now go around the circle, in front of the participants, in a clockwise direction. It is gradually drawn towards the centre of the circle, where it rises and reaches up into the atmosphere to contact all persons, countries and projects mentioned.

Each time the group of healers meets in a circle to send energy, they will add to the energy previously created in the centre of the room. If at any time they need personal support, help or healing, they need only link into the pillar of energy by asking inwardly to do so, and they will receive all they need.

Healing energy is being sent by healers at all times, all over the world. All people benefit from this energy, and when in need they can reach out from their inner self, their spirit, and receive all they require.

Spirit energy group healing

Some healers contract spiritually to participate in healing work whilst asleep. Spirit groups comprising soul energies, plus out-of-body spirits based in physical bodies, join during the sleep time to assist those in need. This work is seldom remembered on waking, and is totally for the benefit of the planet and the people on it, not as an ego boost or lesson-learning for the healer.

These energy groups work in areas such as air, train and shipping disasters. They also visit areas where loneliness, fear and pain are causing torment.

When a person is asleep or near death, their spirit can leave their body. The spirit is able to communicate, whatever the state of the brain or body. As spirits we are able to calm them, to give encouragement and healing energy.

When the spirit is willing and able to leave its body safely, whenever its particular energy is needed, it will link with others, do the work and return to its body afterwards, with absolutely no ill effects. There is no reward, no remembrance, no dream – it is a totally selfless action.

When the spirit of a person has participated in one of these missions, he or she will wake, feeling relaxed, harmonious and peaceful.

Balancing and energising centres

As explained earlier, each centre has its own energy colour. Spirals of energy run from each centre to the next, so that all centres inter-relate. The energy of each centre moves in a clockwise direction.

The energy based in the inspiration centre in the upper head is blue. A blue energy line from this centre moves down to connect and spiral within the communication centre energy. It then moves down to the emotional centre, spirals, moves along the arms to the hands and returns to travel down to the courage centre, where it spirals, then moves down to the creative centre, spirals and moves down the legs, returning to the inspiration centre.

The energy based in the communication centre in the lower head and neck is mauve. From this centre a mauve energy line moves up to inspiration, returns to communication, moves to emotion, spirals, moves along the arms, back through itself to the centre, moves down to courage, spirals, moves down to creativity, spirals, moves down the legs to the feet, and returns to its own centre.

The energy based in the emotions centre is pink laced with red. It moves up to communication, spirals, moves up to inspiration, spirals, returns to emotion, moves down to courage, spirals and moves on to creativity, spirals and moves down the legs to the feet. Then it returns to its own centre.

The solar/courage centre energy, which is yellow, moves up to emotion, spirals, moves to communication, spirals, moves to inspiration, spirals, returns via the centres to courage, then moves down to creativity, into the legs and feet and back to its own centre.

The energy in the creative centre moves up to courage, spirals, moves to emotion, spirals, moves to communication, spirals, moves to inspiration, spirals and returns to the creative centre.

If any centre is unbalanced for any reason, all the other centres are immediately affected because they all inter-relate.

 ## Checking the balance of the centres

Periodically you should check whether the centres are in balance and inter-relating correctly. The patient should be asked to lie down. Stand at the feet of the patient and line up the physical body, adjusting it if it is out of line.

Begin about six inches above the patient's head.

Inwardly tell yourself you wish to tune into the blue of inspiration. Check the blue in its own centre and follow the blue line moving down into the communication centre. Check the blue energy moving through the mauve and down to the emotions centre. Check the blue as it spirals round the centre and then moves down to the courage centre. Check as it spirals around the courage centre and moves down to the creativity centre including the legs and feet.

If at any point you sense an imbalance in the blue energy, pause. Concentrate blue energy from your mid-forehead centre on to the imbalance and hold, until you sense it is moving correctly.

When inspiration (blue) has been traced down and back to its centre, repeat the process with communication (mauve). Check the mauve in its own centre first, then up via inspiration, down to communication, down and round emotion, down and round courage, down and round creativity, including legs and feet, and back to its source centre.

If an imbalance is sensed, pause, then send mauve from your mid-forehead centre to the point affected until you sense the imbalance has been corrected.

The next centre is emotion (pink/red). Carry out the same process as before. Repeat for courage (yellow), then creativity (green).

The nervous centre (tree of life) can be scanned from the front, but some people prefer to work at the back. Turn the person round, back facing you. From a point twelve inches above their head, sense the deep green/blue of the nervous system. Sense the energy line spiralling down the spine to below the feet. Tune into the fine green/blue threads of energy, gently intertwining through all the centres and colour spirals. If any section feels unbalanced, laser in green/blue. These green/blue fern-like threads have a silver tip to them.

Next, from your mid-forehead to twelve inches above their head send a beam of all colours. Sweep down past all centres to below their feet and return to above their head. Switch off the contact by sensing the colours fading. Ask them to stand and shake and stretch in their own space. Move away from the person and brush your hands together to disconnect.

This exercise can also be carried out by using the hands to sense the colours. Place the hands above each centre and, whilst moving the hands slowly down the energy line, sense any fluctuation. Repeat for each centre as above.

The value of gemstones and quartz

Gemstones and quartz are another valuable source of energy, in relation to both the centres and to healing. All stones vibrate and have an energy field surrounding them; its content and use depend on the type of stone and its environment. The energy of the sapphire corresponds to the inspiration centre, which is blue. It helps to lift depression. The amethyst corresponds to the communication centre, which is mauve. Intoxication, dizziness and tension headaches can be relieved by this energy. Rose quartz soothes the emotions, while the ruby balances physical energy. Amber and yellow topaz correspond to the solar/courage centre which is deep yellow at the centre and paler at the outer ring. The emerald energy balances the creativity and progress centre, which is green. It also helps the legs when movement is restricted. Jade and turquoise correspond to the nervous centre, which is located near the spine. They are good for soothing and easing nerves and back pain. The opal energy links into the brain. The brain has all centre colours represented, as it controls all the bodily functions. The multicolour glow surrounds the head. This circle effect around the head is called a halo. The moonstone corresponds to the spirit centre.

By wearing the stone to correspond with the centre in need, its energy can be utilised to balance, cleanse and energise the whole person.

Quartz of any kind releases energy which can be used in healing work.

To energise quartz it should first be cleaned (see page 90) then held by the owner for a few minutes every day. Wrap it in red cloth and then black. The red energy feeds the quartz, while the black cloth stops outside vibrations getting in. Quartz takes up to three months to energise fully, according to its energy loss. If you are unsure, energise for three months.

The energy of quartz will affect people and animals when they are in its vicinity. Quartz is affected by the energies around it. Therefore if it is constantly uncovered near humans in need, it absorbs their energy and will eventually transmit that energy. It is now working in reverse of its healing function. The room will feel uncomfortable and unwholesome as time goes by. So keep quartz covered when not in use. Wash pieces under running water at the end of the day. Hold them and cover them up.

 Colour energy in quartz, stones and glass for healing

The colour content in quartz, clear stones and glass is an aid to healing. Sunlight shining through them is best, but electric light can also release the colours and bathe with energy the person in need.

Sometimes one colour is required to balance a centre. At other times all the centres will need to be treated. Blue in quartz, stones or glass helps to relieve depression and physical pain and to strengthen bones. Red is beneficial for the heart. Pink balances the emotions, yellow aids courage and stability, while green will benefit creativity and progress. A mixture of colours is beneficial for skin disorders. Although glass is not a natural material, as long as the colour is deep and clear it can be used.

A frame can be made with a section for glass of each colour. The colour used should correspond to the centre colour. Sit the person in front of the frame, shine light through the glass and let the colours reflect on them. The coloured light will combine with the energy of the healer who is present.

PART FOUR

Responsibility and psychic sensing

This section is about the responsibility of the psychic practitioner. It also includes various methods and exercises which will help you to develop your psychic abilities.

Responsibility

If you practise as a psychic, you will affect those you work with. Your words and actions can bring about a change in health and also a change in life patterns. You are responsible for what you say.

When working with a client the information is received via pictures, sound, smell, thought patterns and a sense of knowing. Past-life information can also be received. When we relate to the client we sometimes have to interpret symbolic pictures which we are sensing. This interpretation needs to be carried out with great care. Always give the symbol as well as the interpretation to the client.

We relate all we sense to the client in order for him or her to make his or her own choices and decisions. We can tell them about past, present and possible future trends. We encourage them to ask questions when they are unclear about what we are saying.

All carers are responsible for their words and actions and because of the nature of psychic work, people are more inclined to absorb and believe what is said. Therefore, psychics need to be sure they are ready to work with care, compassion and understanding before they work with the public.

All people are responsible for what they do and are involved in. Our actions in the past and present shape our future. A psychic can help others to construct their today to strengthen their tomorrow. When a psychic works in this way, he or she senses what will happen if the person continues in their present way of life and what will occur if they change various aspects. He or she should always give the alternatives if sensed so that the person can choose and make corrections, plan and live life to the full.

Death is unavoidable, and the time is seldom sensed by a psychic. Knowing our death date is not constructive. Most people change drastically when told they will die at a certain time. The purpose of all life is to live it, every day, fully, and with dignity.

Some psychics translate symbols as reality and cause a great deal of pain and confusion. For instance they translate a symbol of an ending as death when it could mean a new beginning; a symbol of 'change' as an illness or disaster. Teenagers told they will die in their twenties have stopped studying and become irresponsible or mentally disturbed. The date they have been given comes and goes, they are still alive, and they have to pick up the pieces and start again, if possible.

The psychic has seen a symbolic ending and the person does end a particular phase at that time. If the person had been given the information as a complete change in life, it could have been an exciting time to plan towards. But by incorrect interpretation it has become a time of destruction instead of construction.

The same doom and gloom can be given to a person by a psychic who perceives an accident or an illness. These can be avoided or lessened in intensity if the information is given correctly and not as an unavoidable situation.

People need our help as psychics because they feel ill, lost or afraid. To add to their distress in unforgivable. If we believe in the right of all humans to be in charge of their own destiny, we will help and encourage them to face up to life by sensing the positive as well as the negative aspects of the choices they are faced with.

Symbols

When using psychic abilities to help a person, the information will be received in many ways. One of them is a symbolic shorthand which can be built up and understood with practice.

Sometimes these symbols will be sensed as pictures, but note should also be taken of things around you or the person you are helping. If you are suddenly aware of a flower in the room, interpret this as a symbol. If a bird sings or becomes obvious, this too is a symbol. If there is a noise which becomes intrusive, that is another symbol and so on. A piece of cotton forming a shape, the grain of wood in the table — these can trigger images. In fact, interpret anything which becomes obvious to you. Do not seek symbols; your psychic sense will pick them up.

Some psychics sense in symbols a great deal, others very rarely, but when they appear they can give you a great deal of helpful information. We all interpret symbols in a totally personal way. Imagination must be controlled; a psychic can tune in to a symbol and be reminded of something that has happened in their own life, which is totally irrelevant. It is essential not to think of yourself when working, for although the interpretation is linked to the psychic's own experiences, what is important is the feeling of the symbol and not the personal connections.

To show how varied symbol interpretation can be, here are a few examples of the different meanings which psychics have for flowers.

Daffodil
Freshness, new beginning, awakening, ending, loss.

Chrysanthemum
Fullness, achievement, sadness, desertion, funeral.

Iris
Celebration, winning, need for healing, deep love.

Awareness

To sharpen your psychic senses, you should sharpen your physical senses. The more alert you are physically, the more alert you will be psychically.

Feel the ground beneath your feet when walking. Feel your clothes on your skin. When you hear sounds, look to see where they come from. Sniff the air and try to identify the scents. Be aware of your surroundings. Thinking of where you have been or where you are going means you have totally missed the experience of the present.

This physical awareness of being in the present means that when you are working psychically you will be totally aware — not thinking, just sensing, speaking and interpreting when necessary. You will achieve a high standard of delivery. Questions and discussions will not interfere with your psychic work, as you will find you can talk and retain your psychic attunement with no interference from yourself and your personal thoughts and opinions.

Clairvoyance

The following exercise is to strengthen the 'seeing' ability known as clairvoyance. It is important for the physical self to be comfortable and unobtrusive when doing psychic work. Personal bodily needs should be attended to before you start.

 Improving your clairvoyance
Sit comfortably, sigh deeply and breathe regularly.

Close your eyes and image in front of you a shut door or a closed window, or even a TV set. Each person will need to find an image which symbolises safety to them — something which can be opened and shut, or switched on and off. I will use the door image.

Please remember that the image you have made is only to give control and remove fear. It is not important in itself, and it can change shape as your psychic ability becomes more active and finds a symbol which may be more suitable to you. Always go with the change, and do not spend time trying to force your image to remain as you made it.

Image the door and open it, sense yourself standing in the doorway and 'look out'. Do not go through the door. Observe; do not think. After two or three minutes, close the door, open your eyes and touch a real object. This part of the exercise is to control your 'seeing'. By opening the door you are indicating that you are willing to see. By closing the door, you are indicating that you no longer wish to see. This trains your psychic sense to activate only when you wish it to do so.

Make a note of what you saw. Do not try to analyse it at this stage.

Image your door again, open it, and sense yourself walking through. Observe what you 'see' and how you feel. Do not try to alter the pictures, as you will then be thinking. If you think, you will start imagining and you will no longer be 'seeing' psychically.

Do not pre-plan, expect or pre-suppose in any way, or once again you will activate your subconscious and imagination and ruin the experience.

After two to three minutes you are ready to return from your 'seeing'. Your door will be in front of you, so there is no need to retrace your steps to find it. Close the door, open your eyes and touch a real object. Make a note of what you saw, but do not try to analyse at this stage.

When you go out of the door in this exercise you are not leaving your body.

The aim of the experience is to teach you to 'see' in depth. The visualisation is actually coming towards you – you are not going to it.

The reason you are asked to touch a real object when you open your eyes is to establish that you are in touch with reality.

You are asked to note down what you saw because a psychic works best if they speak as they receive, interpreting as they go. If they try to remember and 'see' at the same time, they are using their brain which can activate imagination. Trying to remember stops the psychic self from seeing more. To have another person noting what you see, as you relate it, is preferable but not always possible, and a recording machine can be used.

This is the first stage in controlled 'seeing'. As you get used to practising this exercise, you will find you do not need the door. You will tune into the energy when ready and 'see', but whilst you are getting used to 'seeing' you are advised to use the door image.

When this stage is completed, practise relating symbolically and as a reality. A psychic who is in control will only activate when given permission and asked for help. Do not give messages to people who have not asked you for your assistance.

The next stage in the 'seeing' exercise is to specify your reason for seeing. Breathe regularly and ask your psychic self to show you pictures for calmness, upliftment or relaxation, or ask a question and read the symbol to reach the answer. When a person asks your help, you will 'see' for them automatically.

While practising 'seeing', if you see monsters or several eyes looking at you, or become frightened, you should stop immediately. Monsters and demons are from your own subconscious and indicate that you are over-tired and are not seeing psychically. Seeing many eyes looking at you is a sign of strain. If you see one eye of beauty looking at you, it signifies the third eye which is a symbol of your psychic ability.

When you are seeing for another person, you will find that all your psychic senses come into play and you will sense in various ways. Your psychic awareness can expand to include thought patterns, voices and feelings as well as a sense of knowing.

Psychometry

When a psychic touches or comes near a person, they tune into the signals and information recorded on and around the person. It is also possible to tune into the record of objects, buildings, stones, metal — in fact anything which is natural. Stone and metal have a tremendous recording ability. With practice you can tune into that record and translate the signals received.

Some psychics will see this record in pictures and hear noises associated with events that have occurred, or may experience psychically what has occurred near the object. This work is called psychometry. The article being held will have a record of its own existence and what occurred around it within its range of energy, and it will also have a record of any person who has handled it or worn it continuously.

To practise psychometry, place the object in your hands, defocus and let it move around in your fingers. The shape, angles and surface texture will link into its aura record and activate your psychic ability. Relate what you receive.

If the object is a piece of rock, the signs received will

relate to the life of the rock, reaching back hundreds of years. If you feel you are falling, it is a sign that the rock has fallen. All signals received will relate to what has happened to or near the rock.

Rocks and stones also have an energy which is totally their own, and can feel loving, inspiring, calming. This energy attracts people and they get very attached to their 'pet rock'.

If you are holding an object which belongs or belonged to a person and has been worn or well handled, the signals will relate to that person. It is possible to go back many years collecting information about the owners of the items.

If the article turns or stays in the left hand, it is a signal that the past is being tapped. If the right hand is favoured, it is a sign of the present or, on occasion, a projection into the future.

If your eyes seem cloudy, it can mean that the person who owns the object is not seeing clearly, either physically or mentally. If your left ear becomes hot or tingling, or you hear noises, it can mean the person has heard news. Tingling in the right ear can mean they will hear news. If your ear feels pleasantly warm, the news is good. If your nose itches, it can mean they will receive information they have been seeking.

Any emotions you feel are the object owner's emotions; any pains are also theirs. Itching in the feet can be a sign of movement — either physical travel or progress in life. A sensation on the cheek means female; a sensation on the upper lip or chin means male. If the article falls from your hands, it signifies the end of something.

In all psychic work it is very important indeed to speak or write down what you receive as you get it. Trying to remember and see at the same time will allow your thoughts to interfere with your psychic ability.

By practising psychometry, and getting the owner of the

article to tell you honestly if you are right or wrong in your interpretation, you can become very proficient and accurate. It can also help you tune into people who have problems and help find the cause of their trouble.

Psychometry is used for many reasons. Psychics can go into houses and, by touching the walls, know what has occurred in the room. They can hold pieces of stone, pottery and metal dug up by archaeologists and tell them what the whole article looked like and who used it.

They can touch stones in circles, as at Stonehenge, monoliths and ruined temples, and see what they looked like through the ages and what the people concerned with them looked like and used them for. They can hold unidentified objects and know their history and use. The range of uses for this psychic ability is very wide.

Some healers are able to place their finger tips on a distressed person and tell exactly what is wrong physically, what part of them is diseased, and what is needed to make them well.

 Clearing past recordings from objects

This section explains how articles of jewellery, pendulums, crystals and other personal objects can be cleaned of impressions and feelings collected by them. This method does not remove the pictorial record giving the history which is used in psychometry.

Should an article, such as jewellery, now belong to a new owner, the emotional feelings attached to articles from past owners should be cleaned off; the object will then have a record of the present owner. Past events and feeling can cause the present owner to change personality or experience depressions, aches or pain totally unrelated to himself or herself, replayed from the article.

Articles of clothing which have been worn by another person can hold their vibration, which can affect the new wearer. Normal cleaning and washing will remove all record of the past owner.

Cleaning off old vibrations

Inwardly tell yourself you wish to clear old energies. Only use the following cleaning method with articles which are water-resistant. You will need:

- A non-metal dish
- A non-metal sieve or tweezers, or a pair of waterproof household gloves
- A piece of white cotton cloth
- A piece of black cotton cloth (or velvet)

Half fill the dish with water which has been boiled and allowed to cool. Place the articles in the water. Put your hands around the dish, fingers linking if possible, and gently rotate the dish anti-clockwise until the surface of the water swings round. The old energies will leave the objects via the water.

Pause. Then rotate the dish clockwise, again until the surface of the water swings. The object is now clear.

Pause. Without touching the water with your hands, remove the articles from the dish. You can use household gloves, non-metal tweezers or strain the water through a plastic sieve. The dish should not be used again until it has been thoroughly washed.

Without touching the articles with your hands, transfer them on to a piece of white cotton cloth and gently dry them, first with an anti-clockwise and then with a clockwise movement. Transfer the articles on to the black cloth and gently rub them first anti-clockwise and then clockwise.

The objects are now ready for use. They will still retain all pictures of their past, but the vibration will be clear for the new owner to record on.

If the article is not waterproof, or is too big for a dish, instead of the water use a blue cotton cloth anti-clockwise and clockwise, then complete the exercise using the white and black cotton cloth.

Divination

Divination is a way of concentrating your eyes and mind on an object so as to exclude thought and outside interference, thereby allowing your psychic ability to work unhindered. Through the ages physics have used many different articles for this focusing: tarot cards, crystal balls, tea and coffee grounds, fire and flame, sheep's entrails, bones, sand, flowers, earth, the palm of a hand, a glass of water, gemstones — in fact, anything which can induce an unfocused state when it is gazed at for a length of time. The art of divination is to find the method which suits your psychic ability the best.

Tarot cards

Tarot cards are a very ancient divination method. The original tarot are said to be a coded record of the history and likely future of mankind. Unfortunately the originals have been lost and only a vague memory of their content has survived to form the basis of the modern tarot card packs. Any set of illustrated cards will work just as well as a pack based on the originals.

If a psychic reads a tarot card book, the information absorbed will interfere with the psychic ability to sense. To a psychic, each card is totally meaningless unless it triggers off a thread of images when used in relation to a person requiring help.

Tarot cards can be read by non-psychic people who memorise meanings from books on the subject. A psychic will achieve a greater depth and understanding of the person because he or she uses the tarot cards as focal points to activate his or her psychic ability to see and sense. The cards, therefore, change their meaning each time they are used.

A tarot card session should not take more than an hour. An hour in the presence of a developed psychic is very concentrated and will cover what is needed at that time. Using objects as a divination means is called a 'reading'. It is easy for a psychic to sense for a very long time, but the person listening gradually becomes more and more overloaded and therefore benefits less and less.

Using tarot cards

Choose a tarot pack which feels comfortable – shapes and colours are the best indicators. Discard the instruction book and packaging. Keep the cards wrapped in a piece of natural material and do not let anyone else touch them.

Hold the cards periodically and shuffle them, wrapping them up after each handling. Shuffle them whether they are used or not. This makes them an extension of the psychic senses.

Some tarot readers hand their cards to the person they are working with, asking them to shuffle the pack. This can disturb the energy surrounding the cards as the other person leaves their impression on them. Although it does not remain very long, it can interfere with the next person's session if it follows on immediately.

When a person arrives and the cards are to be used, shuffle them, touch hands with the inquirer, shuffle the cards again and lay them out to read them. If a card is upside down, it makes no difference to its meaning.

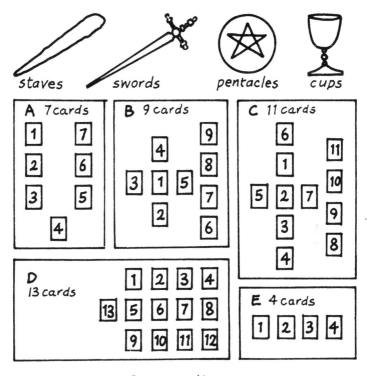

Tarot card layouts

The diagram shows some classic layouts which work well as triggers and take an hour to work through. You will notice that layout A uses seven cards, B nine cards, C eleven cards, D thirteen cards and E four cards. As you complete your reading of each layout, gather the used cards together and place them on one side.

Breathe quietly and deeply to concentrate yourself and ignore all preconceived impressions. Lay out the first set of cards. Let your senses travel over the cards the way you laid them down. Do not stare at them. Sense them. You will find that certain colours stand out or certain parts of a card are more predominant than others. These are the clues to the threads you will follow to help the person. Here are some general guidelines which you might find helpful, but please do not rely on them. Only use them if they are predominant. Read the cards from left to right in the layout. The left is the past, the middle is the present and the right is the future, relating both to the complete layout and to the individual cards. Always read as symbolic and reality, also physical and spiritual.

The staves: In general these relate to business and work matters and are the same as clubs in a normal pack of cards.

The swords: In general these relate to energy and power and are the same as spades in a normal pack of cards.

The pentacles: In general these relate to money and rewards, both of a physical and spiritual nature, and are the same as diamonds in a normal pack of cards.

The cups: In general these relate to emotions, giving and receiving, and are the same as hearts in a normal pack of cards.

On occasions you will find your ability to pick up information for the person activates so strongly that you only need to lay one set of cards to trigger all the psychic senses. Sometimes you will not need the cards at all; only use them if you need the trigger to start your psychic senses working. Avoid relying on the cards. Practise using different types of divination articles so as to be able to work at any time, using anything to hand to focus your mind.

The most important aspect of our work is interpreting what is sensed into acceptable language. After reading the cards from the general view, let your senses travel over each card in turn, relating what you receive as you move around. If you are unable to interpret, ask. Encourage the person to talk. The sound of their voice vibration will give you a closer contact with them. Encourage the enquirer to ask you questions and also to query your answers if they are not understood.

We psychics want the person to contribute — it is their life, their problem, their future choices we are working on. Encourage them to record or note what you are sensing.

If they are writing down your replies, they should also write down their questions. If not, confusion can arise later when they read what you have said and try to remember the questions they asked.

We do well to remember that our basis for doing this work is to clarify and to encourage healing and positive thought in others. Our work helps the person to construct a good path to follow. It is unprofessional, cruel and totally unethical to relate what is received in a purposely negative, destructive fashion.

Use your psychic abilities to read the cards to find the choices the person has, in order to help them choose. Whenever a crisis is foreseen the psychic should also check to see if it can be lessened or avoided. Seek the reasons and possible outcome.

When you have finished reading all the layouts of the cards, gather them together, shuffle them and wrap them up until needed again.

Do not try to remember anything you have seen for a person. Avoid discussing what you have sensed after you have finished the session. You will remember if it is discussed in normal conversation. Forgetting alleviates embarrassing situations should you meet your sitter socially — you could refer to something discussed in the privacy of the sitting.

Crystal balls

These can also be used for divination, although they have many other uses as well.

When not in use, keep it wrapped in black velvet. This

prevents scratch marks and stops light and vibrations entering.

For this work, the crystal ball should be as perfect as possible, since flaws can distract some psychics. It should be wrapped, and handled by the psychic periodically, then re-wrapped, whether used or not. Your energy and the energy of the crystal will then inter-relate and work in harmony.

 ## Using a crystal ball for divination

First clean the crystal ball following the method given on page 90. When the person you are helping has seated himself or herself, unwrap the crystal, touch it, hold the hand of the person, then touch the crystal again. Some crystal users ask their sitters to touch the crystal, but crystals hold vibrations and after each session will need cleaning to clear them. When you are working all day with different people, this becomes too time-consuming. By touching the person and then the crystal you make enough contact to assist you in helping the person, but he or she is not impressed on the energy field of the crystal enough to remain long after the session.

Breathe deeply and clear your mind. Look through the crystal or near it. Do not look at it, as you will not see anything.

The crystal works differently for different psychics. Some see images and symbols within the crystal, others find they are receiving the images within themselves. Some receive better with their eyes shut. Practise to find the way most suited to you.

The crystal energy will tune into the aura of the person and, in conjunction with your psychic energy, reflect the images. That is why some psychics see in the crystal and some within themselves, depending which energy is stronger. Relate with care all that you sense, as already mentioned.

When the images cease, rub the crystal gently clockwise with the velvet, touch it and rewrap it.

Keeping the crystal wrapped is done for reasons of safety, too. If the sun shining into the room concentrates on the crystal, fire can result. The magnification properties of crystal are very strong indeed.

A crystal ball can transmit energy. Even if you do not need to use your crystal at a psychic reading session, you can still unwrap it whilst you are working with a person so that the energy can be released to benefit the person and yourself.

In addition, crystals are used for meditation. Focusing on them for this purpose can induce a deep trance so this practice should be used with great care.

Tea leaves and coffee grounds

Tea leaf and coffee ground readers are not always taken seriously, but this is a valid and non-frightening method of seeing for others. Some people are afraid of tarot cards, crystal balls and so on but are quite happy when a homely teacup is used for divination. Using a cup from which a person has been drinking incorporates psychometry, and the psychic is helped by tuning into the vibration of the drinker still on the cup.

There are books on cup reading which designate parts of the cup for different parts of the life and list what the symbols made by the leaves or grounds mean. However, as with tarot cards, if a psychic reads someone else's ideas on the meaning of things seen, they are interfering with their own natural ability to tune in.

 ## Reading cups

The person being read for should hold the cup of liquid between their hands as they drink until there is a minute amount left in the bottom, with the leaves or grounds floating in it. He or she should swing the cup gently two or three times and turn it upside down into a saucer. The cup is then handed to you, the reader. Hold it upright between your hands and gaze into it.

Some of the leaves or grounds will be at the bottom of the cup and some stuck to the sides. As you gently gaze over them, shapes will become clear — some very obvious and some seen psychically.

Interpret these shapes as you sense them. Avoid the obvious, such as a teapot shape meaning domestic matters, unless that is what you feel. In divination, words, sights and sensations pass through your psychic sense and are related to the enquirer.

The use of leaves and grounds in this way is very valid, and some psychics find this method works better for them than cards or crystals.

 ## Fire and flame

Braziers of burning coal have been used for divination for thousands of years; the glowing coals send the psychic into a semi-trance state very easily. An open fire or camp-fire work in the same way.

After gazing into the flames for a short while, your eyes will glaze over and a daydreaming or defocused state is reached. The images can then be related.

 ## Sand

Place some sand in a box and add a small amount of water to dampen it. Shake the box and ask the enquirer either to impress their palm into the sand or to agitate the sand by stirring it with a finger. Then gaze at the sand and the shapes in it will trigger off the psychic senses. Relate what you sense.

Bones and stones

Some psychics use bones and stones, reading them according to the direction in which they fall. This method is very popular in certain societies. The witch-doctor throws bones on the ground and reads them to resolve problems in the tribe.

 Clothes

Another method of divination is to gaze at the folds and creases of the clothes the client is wearing. Using this method, the person's left is their past, their right is the future.

Defocus and allow your psychic senses to pick up from the way the person is sitting, how their sleeve creases, whether the crease goes up or down; if their collar is flat or crumpled; sense from lines and images formed by the folds in the cloth and interpret as you tune in. You may feel, for instance, that, if the end of their collar has turned and is now appearing as an arrow head pointing to the right, they are pushing forward to the future; or if their left sleeve is creased and in shadow, but their right sleeve is smooth and in light, that their future is going to ease out and be more manageable due to clarity. If they are sitting on their right foot, you could sense they are restricting their future progress.

Use these clues to help you to tune into their energy. Remember, it is the psychic sensing which enables this to occur — it will not happen if you are unconnected to the person.

 Postcards

Purchase a selection of postcards, choosing pictures which are colourful. Shuffle them and ask the enquirer to choose one. Take the chosen card in your hand and interpret the angles, shadows, colours and shapes as your eyes gently roam over the picture. Remember left is the past, right is the future. Your psychic ability will select what is appropriate.

 ### Photographs

A photograph of a person, with background detail, can be read in a similar manner. Any photograph will do; its age does not matter.

Hold the photograph in your hand and let your eyes roam over the surface. Certain shadings, angles, and the position of the main figures will all help you tune in and then relate what you perceive.

Pendulums

A pendulum is an extension of your psychic self, an outward sign of what you are tuning into. It can be made of anything but usually works better when made of natural materials. It consists of a weighty object suspended from a cord or chain.

Either hand can be used to hold the cord and suspend the pendulum, which should hang from the back of the index finger. If the pendulum is held between the thumb and finger, the pulses at the ends of those digits can interfere and cause the pendulum to swing.

When you have made or found your pendulum and feel it suits you, the next stage is to establish the method it will use to show 'yes' or 'no'. Suspend it over your index finger, hold it over your left palm and ask: 'Is this my left hand?' Whichever way the pendulum swings is positive or 'yes'. Then hold it over the right palm and ask the same question: 'Is this my left hand?' The way the pendulum swings will mean negative or 'no'.

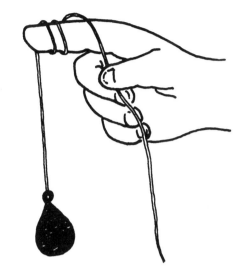

Using a
pendulum

All pendulums should be checked for 'yes' and 'no' as they can combine circular movements and swing movements. It is unwise to assume that if a pendulum swings in a clockwise direction for 'yes' it will swing anti-clockwise for 'no'. Each pendulum you use will have its own way of showing positive and negative, and you should always check for them.

For accuracy it is important to abide by some rules:

1 Never let another person touch your pendulum.

2 Keep it in a small pouch on its own and carry it near your body.

3 Do not use your pendulum when other people are near. They can affect the answer it gives.

4 Never use the pendulum twice by repeating the question, or ask for an answer when it is already known.

5 If you have a shock or emotional upset in your life, you

should check for positive and negative again as a pendulum can change if you change.

6 Fill your head with the question so that no other thought can intrude.

7 Do not use it to make decisions you could make for yourself.

Here is the thinking that lies behind this list of rules. First in order for your psychic energy to use the pendulum, it needs your energy on and around it. If another person touches it, or uses it, it will have their energy on it. Your accuracy can be impaired by this other energy.

By keeping your pendulum in a small pouch near you, it will absorb your energy. It then becomes part of you.

If you use your pendulum whilst another person is nearby, their thoughts can influence it. A person who desperately wants a particular answer can be sending out an intense energy, and the pendulum can be moved by their thought pattern. If a person calls out a question whilst you are using your pendulum, even if they are talking to someone else and you are not involved, your pendulum will answer their question, not the one you are asking. Pendulum work is private and needs your complete concentration.

If you check an answer given by your pendulum, you are checking your own abilities and putting out a doubting vibration which can cause an opposite second answer. Also, if you know that the enquirer is already in possession of the information being asked, you will send out a vibration based on fear of being wrong and that will affect the pendulum — the answer will be wrong or confused.

The pendulum can become so sensitive to your vibration that, should you be deeply hurt, physically or emotionally, it too will feel shock; just as you feel out of harmony, so will your pendulum. It can work in reverse when this happens, so it must be checked for positive and negative movements. The pendulum will give a true 'yes' or 'no' on checking because you are not being tested and will not interfere with fear of failure. When you are ready to ask the question, repeat it over and over in your head to exclude all other thoughts. If another question creeps in, the pendulum will answer that one. For example, if you were using your pendulum to ascertain an allergy to a food and you suddenly wonder if you have locked your car, the pendulum can move 'yes' or 'no' to tell you about the car, not about the food allergy.

It is unwise to use any method of divination to replace your own responsibility. Asking the pendulum if you should do A or B is irresponsible if you have not tried to work out the answer yourself. Some people get so addicted to their pendulum that they are unable to make any decisions without it. Pendulums should only be used after you have tried to make a choice by thought, logic, psychic ability or common sense. If you ask it a personal question, your mind (knowing what you subconsciously want the answer to be) can interfere.

However, if you really cannot make a choice and the pendulum is the last resort, you would be wise to place six cards in six identical envelopes. On one card write 'yes' and on another write 'no'. The other cards should remain blank. Mix the envelopes up so you cannot know which ones have the 'yes' and 'no' cards in them, then ask your question. If you are to have the answer, the pendulum will move over the envelope which has an answer card in it. If it moves over an envelope which has a blank card in it, you are not going to get your answer by using the pendulum.

Pendulums can be used in many situations. If you feel you are allergic to a certain food, but cannot find which one it is, place samples of your food on a table and hold your pendulum over each one asking: 'Is this good for me?' or

'Am I allergic to this?' The pendulum can give you the answer.

Once you have been informed that you are allergic to particular foods, whether by the pendulum or some other means, you can use your pendulum once a week to ascertain if your allergy has passed. Similarly, if you have been told to eat a certain food, you can use your pendulum once a week to ascertain if you still need that particular food. The body is constantly changing and what you need, or do not need, one week can be changed completely as your body changes.

If it is not possible to have samples for the pendulum to work over, it will still work if you write the words on paper instead. Some psychics can just fill their mind with the thought of the article and get a reply.

Pendulums can also give the time of a person's birth if it is not already known. It will also indicate where lost articles, people or animals are. It will even help you find lost or unknown items in a house or garden.

 How to find a birth time

Make a chart of twelve squares. Place a number in each square. Starting at the top left-hand square write the figure 1, then in the next square write 2, and so on along the top row. Continue along the next row down until you have the numbers one to twelve in separate boxes. On the same page as this chart, put 'a.m.' in one box and p.m. in another box. This chart is for the hour of birth. On another piece of paper, make another chart of 59 squares and put one number in sequence in each box. This chart provides the minutes past the hour the person was born. (See diagram).

When using your pendulum for another person, it will help if you have their photograph, their name written by them on a piece of paper, or an article personal to them.

Place the hour chart plus the personal object on a clear, clean table. Touch the article with the pendulum and hold

a.m.			
1	2	3	4
5	6	7	8
9	10	11	12
p.m.			

Hour Chart

it over the a.m. box. Ask if the person, using their name, was born a.m. Then hold the pendulum over p.m. When that answer has been ascertained, hold your pendulum over each numbered box in the chart, asking if the person was born one o'clock, two o'clock etc. until you get a reaction. Next, remove the hour chart and place the minute chart on the table. Hold the pendulum over each box on the minute chart and ask which minute the person was born. When you get a reaction, you have their birth time.

◎ *How to find missing people, animals or objects*

You need a photograph, personal article or (for people) a sample of their handwriting, a map of the country where

1	2	3	4	5	6	7	8	9	10
11	12	13	14	15	16	17	18	19	20
21	22	23	24	25	26	27	28	29	30
31	32	33	34	35	36	37	38	39	40
41	42	43	44	45	46	47	48	49	50
51	52	53	54	55	56	57	58	59	

Minute Chart

they were last seen and a grid of squares drawn on see-through paper.

Place the personal article on the table, put the grid over the map, touch the article with your pendulum and, holding the pendulum over each square in turn, ask where the person is. When you get a reaction in a particular square, get a larger-scale map of that area; place the grid over the map and repeat the process. You will now have a specific area. If you can get a street map of the area, repeat on that map. You now have the location.

You will find where they are at the time of using the pendulum. If they have moved on when the location is visited, use the pendulum again.

Indoor prospecting can also be carried out using your pendulum. For example, draw a map of your garden, place the grid over the drawing and ask if there is gold in the area, then silver and so on. You will get a reaction in the relevant square if the metal is present in the garden. Get a spade and dig to find the object.

You can find lost articles inside and outside the home by drawing the room or area in which you believe the article to be, placing the grid over the drawing and asking your pendulum where the article is.

Sitting quietly with your pendulum and grid, you can find things anywhere in the world. If a person in another country asks you to find missing things, all you need is a map of the area with your grid and pendulum and you can find the answers for them.

 ## How to find ley lines

Ley lines are the energy lines of the earth (see also p. 164). To find ley lines in relation to a house, draw a map of the house and surrounding area. Hold the pendulum over the top left corner and ask inwardly to be shown ley lines. The pendulum will swing in the direction of the ley line. Draw the swing on your map and continue until all the map has been covered. You will now have a pattern of ley lines, if there are any, drawn on the map. Hold the pendulum over each of the lines you have drawn in turn and ask if there is water present. If you get a reaction along a particular line, draw it in with another colour.

 ## Using hands or fingers in place of a pendulum

Some psychics are able to use their hand or finger instead of a pendulum. Their sensitivity is so fine that they get a reaction in their finger tips or palms when the correct answer has been found. If you use this method you should wash your hands immediately before the work and again afterwards to ensure there is no interference from outside energies in your hand area.

 ## Crystal pendulums for healing

Pendulums made of crystal are used mainly for healing and energy work. Crystal has an energy of its own and is best used for diagnosing, correcting imbalance and confirming energy flows.

The crystal pendulum should be kept in its own pouch. No one else should use it, of course. After you have used it over a patient it should be cleaned in running water, held by you and replaced in its pouch. As with all pendulums, suspend it from the back of the index finger.

The patient should lie down. Hold the pendulum a few inches from the top of their head and slowly move it down their body. You will find the pendulum will react over a negative energy area. Suspend the crystal over that area and it will correct the imbalance with its own energy linked into your healing energy. When the pendulum stops moving, or moves in the positive way, you can move on down the body. Some healers find the patient's imbalance with the crystal, then use their own hands to correct it, using the pendulum afterwards to confirm that harmony and balance have been restored.

Dowsing

From my research I have found that in every group of people there will be someone who can find concealed water by the technique known as dowsing. Water is essential to survival, and when humans are in danger from lack of it the survival instinct will activate in one of them. A person who could dowse for water was very important in bygone times and with practice became very adept. It was considered a gift from God, so others who could have done the same never tried.

A psychic can dowse for anything at any time. You need a dowsing instrument, which can be made of wood, metal or other natural materials. The shape of the rod and the most appropriate material have to be selected by the individual doing the dowsing: what suits one will not suit another.

Obviously the rod is very personal to the owner, as with pendulums, and should not be passed around and handled by others. Some dowsers have different rods for finding different things.

One type of rod is made by placing together two pieces of wire, about 20 inches long, and twisting the ends for a third of the total length, so the twisted end becomes the pointer. A Y-shaped piece of tree is an old method, the single twig being the pointer while the two side arms are held by the dowser. Two strong metal rods with the ends bent over for easy handling can also work well. These rods are left single, so no spring action is possible. They are held one in each hand pointing forward.

Having made your dowsing rod, you need to get a strong tension. By pulling the wire apart and down you will get a good spring movement. Hold the rod horizontally, directly in front of you, and walk at a steady pace, gently moving it from side to side.

The person dowsing has to be able to concentrate fully. When other people are present it is advisable that the dowser moves in front of them and they follow some feet behind.

If you are searching for water, fill your mind with an image of water and repeat the word 'water'. If you are searching for gold, fill your mind with an image of gold and repeat the word 'gold'. When the rod has found the requested item, it turns and twists up and down very strongly. For some dowsers it reverberates.

Dowsing rods are very good for locating underground pipes carrying electricity, gas or water. The rod will continue to activate while you follow the pipeline in question. Ley lines too can be tracked in this way. When dowsing outside for pipelines or ley lines, it is advisable to have a companion marking the ground with rocks or markers behind the dowser so the line is visible.

Some psychics dowse with their feet and have no need for a rod. Their feet tingle, burn or swell when the required item, or line, has been found.

Doodles

Doodles are fascinating and common to all. When made by psychics, they can be translated and used to help a person or to gain understanding. Any doodles which you do all the time are not relevant for this exercise.

The doodle is an outward sign of what you, the psychic, are picking up from the person you are listening to. The doodle refers to the person talking; the only time the doodle is for you, the doodler, is if you are sitting alone and your thoughts are personal.

Paper and pen by the telephone will ensure you can doodle whenever your hand wants to, during a conversation. If you realise you are doodling you will think about it and your mind will interfere. When this happens, stop doodling and translate what you already have.

Doodles come in various shapes and sizes: some cover a large area while others are minute. Some are symbolic and some reality, or they can be a combination of both.

The first thing to do when you realise you have a doodle is to gaze at it. If it is a rambling doodle and covers the paper, you can divide it by creasing the paper into three sections vertically. The left is the past, the middle the present, the right the future. Crease the paper horizontally across the middle. The bottom half is material and physical, the top half spiritual and mental. If the doodle is too small to divide, translate it as a whole.

If you are interviewed for a job and find you have doodled while listening to the interviewer, your doodle will tell you a great deal about the person and how honest they have been about the job. If you are the interviewer, your doodle would tell you about the interviewee. Doodling at a lecture or speech session will tell you about the speaker and their true feelings about their subject.

Doodling while 'reading' will give you additional helpful information. Practice helps develop the ability. If you doodle while speaking to a friend, interpret the doodle and ask the friend to assess the accuracy. Some psychics find that a doodle they have drawn is in fact a real place. These psychics can use their ability, when asked to find missing persons, by holding the person's jewellery, clothing and so on and doodling a picture of where the person can be found.

Dreams

Whilst we are awake, our brain is continually being bombarded with images, smells, sounds, tastes, new ideas, emotions, and so on. All that happens every minute of our life has to be sifted and filed appropriately. But when the brain is fully occupied, protecting and monitoring the body and its functions, it cannot immediately file everything that is happening. So it stores certain items until the body sleeps, when further attention can be given to sorting out and filing this temporarily housed information.

If this sorting procedure is stopped because the person is unable to sleep, the brain becomes stressed. This leaves the person in a very traumatic state, mentally and physically.

Some dreams are the events of the day running through the brain for sorting purposes. Sometimes the events overlay each other and the dream is a confused mixture of many images.

We all dream, but not all dreams are remembered. Sometimes we recall odd mixed fragments, sometimes the complete dream is recalled. There are many books written about translating dreams and many therapists who work on this subject.

Psychics interpret dreams which stand out for their brightness of colour, intensity and impact. These include spiritual messages, past life recall, travelling and visitors. We also translate dreams to obtain insight on the dreamer's hidden fears and problems. A dream can give a factual report or a symbolic picture, or combine fact and symbol.

There are certain common images which translate the same for many of us. Water which appears in a dream, but seems to have no relevance to the content, can be a sign that the dream is spiritually inspired. Black can denote the inner spiritual self, white the physical outer self. A dream of black and white squares, for instance, shows the balance in a person. Finally, dreams can be translated using left for the past and right for the future.

Recurring dreams

Dreams which recur can be preparation for a future event. If the dream is interpreted correctly so that its message is understood, it will stop. Recurring dreams can also be a sign of worry and confusion. Interpreting the dream helps the person face the problem and understand it.

Out-of-body dreams

All people have a spirit which can leave its body whilst it sleeps. Some do this on rare occasions, others very frequently. A dream of flying, being in another country or talking to another person you know is far away are all likely to be out-of-body memories. A sudden waking with a heart jump and/or a dream of falling or spiralling down, is a sign that a spirit has been out of its body whilst it sleeps. Out-of-body travel is discussed in greater detail on p.131.

Past life dreams

A person may remember a dream where they were living in a strange bygone time, wearing clothes from another century or even speaking a language they no longer understand. This is usually a sign that they have linked into one of their own past lives to regain knowledge by re-experience to help them in their present existence.

On some occasions, on waking they recall that they were in the past but as an observer of what was occurring. These observing dreams are to remind and recall a past life, but without the need to re-experience it.

You should listen carefully so as to assist the person find the link with present problems. Some psychics can link into the life related and obtain further information to help the person.

Information dreams

Some people go to sleep with questions or problems they cannot resolve. These dreams usually appear in a symbolic form which, when interpreted, will help them find the answers they need. It is possible to repeat a specific question in the mind just before going to sleep, and then dream the answer.

Visitors/visiting dreams

Out-of-body spirits can visit a sleeping person and communicate via the spirit consciousness. The person visited will recall a feeling of someone having been in the room, and half remember conversations. It is possible, if we are worried about a person on earth, to ask our spirit to visit them.

Many of these dreams occur just before waking, usually between three and five in the morning. In fact, some people are quite convinced they were awake during the whole experience.

When the spirit returns you wake up because you are dehydrated. Out-of-body activity uses energy and the body fluids. It is advisable to place a drink by your bed each night and, when you wake at this early hour, sip it without disturbing your body too much. You will then go back to sleep.

Those of you who find it hard to recall dreams on waking

can train yourselves to do so. Put a pad and pencil near your bed so that you can reach it easily. When you wake in the early hours, with the remembrance still present, avoid any thinking but just reach out and write down everything you can. If you allow your thought processes to begin you will activate your brain and immediately start forgetting.

When you have written what you can, sip your drink and return to sleep. In the morning you will find your scribbled words on your pad and will be able to recall some of the memory of the dream. Even if you have had another dream, you will still remember something. If you get into a habit of writing down your dreams in this way, you will gradually retain more until you have complete recall in the morning. Keep a dream log for reference.

The brain is very good at filing away normal, everyday events but has difficulty in filing events which are not related to physical living. The psychic events and spirit trips which occur during sleep are not received in the same way as reality. The brain will accept them more easily for recording if you write down what you remember and read it back to yourself; the information will be recorded as a story or a detached event. Gradually, as you write and read your dream memories, your brain will absorb the material instead of wrapping it up in a dream of everyday matters in order to file it away.

Premonition

Psychics can receive premonitions of future events at any time, awake or asleep. Usually only premonitions of disasters are remembered, as they make such an impact. Information can be received in advance about floods, volcanoes erupting, plane and train crashes, death by violent means of a well-known person, a famous building collapsing, a war, fire in a public place and multiple deaths. These impressions are not messages to particular psychics, transmitted so that they can act to avert the disaster. They have not been chosen to save a section of humanity. What impressions are is advance vibrations of an inevitable event. Psychics are very sensitive to atmosphere — some are so sensitive that they pick up these vibrations like television signals and translate them into pictures. The event cannot be changed, as the vibration received is already recorded on the atmosphere and the cause unchangeable.

Most of these impressions are vague and incomplete, and the information insufficient to pinpoint the event. The impressions can be received days, weeks or months before, and there is usually no way to put a date on the premonition from the information received. Some psychics, however, receive premonitions often enough to work out from personal past experience when they are likely to occur.

Remember, if you should tune into world events and have a premonition of disaster, it is not personal to you and other psychics will have sensed it too, in greater or lesser detail. It is not given to you so that you can do something about it. You are tuning into the vibrations in the atmosphere. If you do have a time pattern and the details are precise so that a place can be pinpointed, the best you can do is warn people so that they can remove themselves from danger. Those who should not be present will take heed, while those who choose to be involved will disregard your warning or stay to help others. Do not get upset and traumatised because of lack of information or of place and time details. There is nothing you can do and you are not being asked to do anything. Record details of the premonition, and the date and time it was received, so as to check your facts and accuracy for future occurrences.

Premonitions about friends or family can be given to them if the knowledge you have is clear, precise and usable. Do not give half-impressions of doom and disaster to an individual. You could cause them to become nervous and have an accident they might have avoided.

Sounds and voices

Many people report hearing voices in the air near them, usually when they are alone. They can hear:

- A voice giving instructions or orders
- A conversation between two or more people
- Edge-of-crowd noise
- Abusive, obscene or violent language
- Names being called
- Music

The majority of this communication comes from the multitude of voices relayed through the atmosphere via television, radio and telephone. If they turn on the television or radio when this happens, the conversation can often be heard. Some plays are violent and include shouting and name-calling. There is always music on the air; we often sing a song and then hear it when we switch on the radio. It is very important that every person takes responsibility for what they transmit, either as a person or via air waves, since their words can affect many people, making their minds disturbed and fearful even though they have turned off the TV or radio.

All vibrations affect all people whatever and whoever they are. Some psychics usually called 'mediums' can hear messages, some of which can come from the spirits of people who have died.

Light trance

Early in the morning, when half awake, many people find they receive, see and sense much more clearly. Some tune into world events, or find that they have poetry, ideas for books, quotes and profound knowledge complete in their mind. Others awake with memories of a beautiful painting and know how to capture it all on paper or canvas; or hear wonderful music.

As soon as we think, we become conscious, and the majority of what we have received is lost. This is because, with thought, our brain has activated. The brain records all things received by its physical senses, while spiritual material is received by the inner senses. The brain can sometimes manage to record parts of what has been received, but much of it is lost and, although the wonder of the revelation is retained, frustration can be experienced at the loss of words, detail and images. Practise keeping the light trance you are in. Refuse to think; just gently write down what you can. Do not try to remember, but let the words and images flow; record them with minimum movement and effort. If you have a recording machine near your bed, quietly speak and record all that you are experiencing. If you can get used to recording as you experience, you will retain much more.

When psychics are working with people they are in a light trance condition, and can return to a fully aware state at any time. They can hear what they are saying without interfering with their own thoughts and, if they find they are losing touch and control, they can adjust immediately by focusing sharply on the other person and touching some article of reality, such as a table. In this state, the mind is less active and the psychic sense more acute. The psychic will be speaking quite normally, conversing with the client.

Automatic writing

Some people receive information via writing, the source of which, they feel, is totally detached from themselves. This usually begins when the person is engrossed in an activity such as reading a book, listening to someone speak or even watching television. Obviously paper and pen have to be on hand for this to happen. Some will be writing or typing when they find themselves putting down words totally different from those they intended. Poems, stories, spiritual wisdom, historical facts and music are all possible through automatic writing. Different communicators will have different handwriting content, and each will be recognisable as a different source.

Most automatic writing is seen after it has happened — the writer realises that words have appeared and has no recollection of putting them on paper. Once this method of receiving has occurred, the writer can purposefully sit with writing implements, breathing slowly, totally detached, and allow the writing to flow.

If you wish to try this method of contact, sit down and place a pen and some paper near your hand. Breathe in slowly, stating your willingness to contact. When your hand begins to move and write, do not look or you will interfere with your mind and imagination. Wait until the writing stops, and only then investigate. When you are able to control your mind, you will be able to watch as your hand writes.

At first it is normal to get rows of loops, then the occasional word. Finally, with patience, you will get sentences written in proper script — different contacts writing in different ways and even in languages unknown to you.

If you use a typewriter, the same principle applies. Breathe in slowly, state your willingness to communicate, and allow your fingers to tap at the keys without thought or interference.

Now, a few words of warning. This method of contact should be checked very carefully. It is possible that your own subconscious is writing. It can be that you are writing what another living person is thinking or even writing. If you watch what you are writing, your imagination can take over and write what you want. A past life memory of your own could be communicating. Should you receive any message purporting to come from a person who is no longer alive, you should ask inwardly for their birthplace and birth or death dates and other checkable information. Check the facts before accepting the message as genuine.

Should the message seem to come from a highly evolved being, check to ensure that the content is fresh and clear and not something you have read or heard before. A message from these sources is usually very factual, wise and to the point. It can indicate imbalance and disharmony in our physical and spiritual lives and offer guidance and help to correct them.

PART FIVE

Past lives and out-of-body travel

This section relates to past lives and reincarnation. Many people have been told that past lives are the cause of their relationship imbalances, traumatic experiences and unhappiness in this life. It is my belief, gained from many years of study and intunement with my inner and higher self, that this theory is not a true one and that each past life is complete and is recorded by our soul as experience, knowledge and wisdom gained. I have included a chapter on sensing past lives for positive reasons. Also included in this section is a chapter explaining out-of-body travel (which is also known as 'astral travel').

 Past lives

A great many people believe in reincarnation and actively seek proof of past life experience. As I see it we have all experienced hundreds of physical lives. They are all recorded on the soul record and are a part of the overall memory of the soul. Past lives form a large part of soul experience. The essence of them all, combined with the soul's natural progression, is the total being, the complete soul.

Each life is a new adventure. Each time the spirit energy comes to earth it retains the personality of the soul and the level of evolution the soul has reached. On arrival, the spirit has to rely on what can be achieved here via a physical life on earth, incorporating a physical inheritance. As complete earth beings we experience adversity and joy while trying to complete the adventure of life on earth with the minimum of suffering and the maximum happiness and harmony. The new life begins with a clean sheet; each past life is considered complete. Some people trigger memories of their soul existence and feel lost and homesick for something they cannot properly understand.

Past lives of psychics have often been spent in civilisations where their abilities were used and valued, and it is usual to sense them as Ancient Egyptians, Orientals, Red Indians, Zulus, representatives of shamans, priests, priestesses, monks, nuns and medicine people − in fact, those types of lives and backgrounds where being psychic was an asset or allowed the person to work without fear.

When past life figures show in the aura they are often called 'guides'. However, as the aura is a personal record of soul, spirit and physical, everything seen is personal.

On the earth we are spirit energy living in a physical body. When the body dies, the spirit is released and returns to its soul. Before it is able to be accepted and unite with its soul, it will clear any unacceptable actions from its last earth existence.

The spirit records on the aura all that it is involved in whilst on earth. On its return to its soul it will experience a replay of the last life for assessment by its soul. Unacceptable actions, whether purely personal or linked to other people, have to be understood and cleared. The spirit senses all it has been involved in during its physical life, and is given opportunities to connect with all those affected by its physical actions whilst on earth in its last life.

It is important to live life with care and understanding in order to return to our soul as clear as possible. Time is of no importance in the soul dimension, and a spirit energy can wait for someone to return to their soul at the death of their physical body many earth years later to meet, correct and clarify, thereby hoping to obtain understanding of last life behaviour which affected them both. This connection can also be made during sleep. After having a dream, a person will relate how he or she met and talked with a person who had died who harmed them in life. In the dream they try to reach an understanding. If understanding is reached, both will feel free.

We have all had many past lives, some close together, some far apart. We do not return to relive past lives. Our past is part of experience and makes us what we are. We cannot go backwards. The only time a past life is relevant is as a helpful memory.

Some people use a real or imagined past life experience as an excuse for unacceptable behaviour in this life. Others accept a traumatic life experience in the belief that they are clearing a past life when they caused grief to others. It is also said that if a person was deprived in one life, the depriver will be the giver this time.

None of these ideas is spiritually based. There is no

excuse for suffering or unacceptable behaviour, whether it be to ourselves, others or the planet. All that we do and say, and the way we affect the living experience of others, is in the now, and responsibility for all our actions is totally ours.

Life on earth is not an ongoing horror story of spirits going round in circles, desperately trying to clear errors from the past. Life is wonderful. We are here from choice. The planet is beautiful and it is an honour to live on it. When the combined consciousness of the human race elevates to its great potential, when each person takes responsibility for their existence, then the spirit of the planet will refine and all life will benefit and evolve.

Many people are interested in their past lives. Some are keen to know if they were famous or are recorded in history. These people should take care not to try to build up their present importance and ego on past life achievements. Right up to their dying day many people do not experience the present as the person they are, having completely neglected the life they have now by living in the past.

Some people go to a place or feel a vibration from another person which can trigger past life memories. These memories are shrugged off and quickly forgotten by most people. But some — usually those who like attention or are unhappy with themselves — make a great deal of fuss about them and even try to repeat an experience as if it concerns another person they are attracted to, using the past life memory as a reason or excuse for their behaviour.

On occasions, a past life memory is recalled because we need the experience to save us repeating mistakes. These memories occur in a dream or after reading a line in a book, or are triggered by something we see or hear.

When a person comes to a psychic for help, the psychic will use his or her ability to ascertain the cause of the trouble. Usually the cause can be found in the person's present life, but on occasions a memory from a past life activates to help them now. The past life is not the cause, but can contain insights.

Sometimes a place or a word can trigger a past life memory but have no message content. In this life we can trigger a memory of childhood by experiencing something familiar from that time. Past life recall can be just the same. A person whose present life is dull, or who feels unimportant, can trigger a memory of a past life when they were important and completely change their personality, partially living a life they have already had and losing contact with the reality of the present. Others are interested in their past lives because they need a root on which to base their present life, finding a lack of purpose in their present without knowledge of their far past. Yet others wish to know their past lives out of curiosity and a need for knowledge of themselves.

When meeting a person who gives you strong reason to believe you have known them in a past life, proceed with care. Just because you have had a past life encounter, it does not mean you need a present life involvement. Some people feel such strong vibrations when meeting a person that they believe it must be a past life connection and for that reason begin a physical relationship. Many of these relationships do not last or can be very difficult. They can collapse because, if they did have a past life together, it has already occurred; we cannot repeat a life we have already had, as our physical and spirit selves cannot be the same twice. A psychic can explain the role of past lives before sensing them and giving the information to the person.

Certain types of hypnosis have been known to take the memory of a person back in time to experience one of their past lives. This is known as regression.

There are obvious benefits in relating a past life to a person as opposed to regressing them, although some people prefer to re-experience for themselves. The psychic can tune into a specific life relative to the need of the person, and however traumatic that life was, the person will gain from the knowledge and experience, not relive the horror.

Some lives have been very traumatic and painful. The spirit was happy to complete its earth life and return to its soul to understand and clarify the experience. If a person is taken back through a regression process, not knowing which life they are going to tune into, they can re-experience all the physical horrors without the understanding of the later soul assessment. The past life can become a part of their present consciousness, which can cause great distress in the present.

It is also possible, in this type of regression, for the person to pick up a past life of the regressor or someone else in the room, and report it as their own, or report a subconscious desire to be someone they admired. This could even be a character from a book, and the person may relate the story of their favourite character as their own in a past life.

When a psychic senses past lives for another person they, and not the person, sense what happened as a detached observer. The person receives the information without the trauma and it is accepted by the brain for programming as information.

Using childhood as an example: it is one thing to know we were unhappy and badly used as a child, and as an adult, to seek help to come to terms with what happened, but another thing entirely to be taken back to that childhood to re-experience it all over again as a present reality.

When a psychic tunes into a person's aura for information to help them, he or she sometimes pick up past lives of the person without necessarily meaning or needing to. If an image is sensed behind or very near a person, within their aura field, it is a past life memory of that person, or a memory of someone whom they know who has died.

The tendency for past life images to appear in this way has caused a great deal of confusion. Some people call them 'guides', a separate entity to help us. Any spirit which has returned to its soul will remain as a part of that soul until the need arises for a rebirth. It will not connect to a person on earth as a spirit entity for the duration of another's earth experience. Our soul chooses to have its spirit energy on earth to carry out a physical existence, to make choices and contribute to life as a whole, not to be influenced by other soul energies.

To believe that the energy of another soul is constantly with us, telling us what to do and how to choose, makes the physical experience meaningless. We all have free will, and part of growth is to understand and use it well. Delegating our responsibility to another, whether physical or spirit, negates that experience. We all naturally tune into our own soul for help and guidance when we need it, and can then choose whether or not we wish to follow the help given. Our own soul is our true helper.

We can seek help from others once we have tried ourselves to overcome the difficulty we are faced with. But if we constantly delegate and do not try to clear our own path we feel lost, always seeking outside and never in contact with our own inner self.

When turning inwards for help, the first source is our physical life knowledge. Next we contact our spirit. If this knowledge is insufficient, the next source of help is our soul, and its record of past experiences, knowledge and wisdom. When this occurs some people have the impression they are communicating with a 'guide', because they have been told that this is so. In fact they are tuning into their own wisdom, physical, spirit or soul; they can even receive the knowledge direct from a specific past life memory, sensing themselves in that life as the person they were.

Some people put the image of the 'guide' whom they have been told they have on to the essence they are sensing. Instead of accepting the help and energy, they allow imagination to take over.

Any help we receive will be to assist us to choose – no spirit energy or soul will tell us what to do. We will meet people, find books, hear news and be given clues, but we have to make the decision ourselves.

Asking for help whilst doing everything we can to help ourselves is like knocking on a door. There will always be someone, whether on earth or our inner self, who will open the door for us. Make a positive effort and you will receive positive help.

The following procedure will help you tune into the past lives of other people for historical facts, curiosity or information to help them.

 ## Sensing past lives

Sit comfortably with the person opposite you. Touch hands to make contact.

Breathe slowly. As you breathe, sense the person's energy field and reach out to them with your psychic senses. Defocus and clear your mind.

Past lives can be sensed in various ways. The psychic may see the enquirer's face contours change, a beard appear, a hat, a collar and so on. When you see any change at all, hold on to the change and you will sense other details of face and clothing.

As you get more practised, you can sense the place they lived in, hear them speak, and, on occasions, feel their happiness or fear. Relate all you get to the person as you get it. Always speak as you receive. It takes practice to see and relate past lives without allowing imagination to add details.

It is important to say exactly what you are getting. Do

not embroider or guess. For instance, unless you can identify a particular time in history you should not try to give a date. The clothes worn can be a clue to time and place. Do not guess at a country unless you can see place names and recognise a landmark or a language.

When you find you are trying too hard, you should stop. The past life should flow easily with the psychic observing or experiencing. If you have to think, you are in danger of imagination taking over.

Some people had a past life where they were close to someone of importance. The more involved they were, the more details they will have recorded about that other person. They can trigger the memory of their own past life and believe they were the important person, even knowing details about that person which make it appear true. When a psychic senses that past life, he or she will ascertain if the person he or she is reading for was an observer or the famous person in question. This is one reason why many people have strong feelings that they were Napoleon, Solomon, Cleopatra, Jesus and so on in a past life. During their life there was only one of each person, but many observers.

To see your own past lives you can use the door method of seeing, related on p.84. Ask to see a past life of your own before opening your door. You can then observe yourself as you were. It is possible to see the face of one of your past lives looking over your shoulder when looking into a mirror. This usually occurs when the room is in semi-light.

When you have finished a session of past life work, you may feel slightly unreal. Drink, and then touch a solid object to bring you back to the present.

Humans have been on this planet for many thousands of years and have had many, many lives. We usually see past lives going back a few centuries, but we can also go back thousands of years. Official records go back many years and a past life can sometimes be verified by research. The clothes, architecture and historical events observed can, on many occasions, be checked for authenticity.

When working on past lives, see if the general feel of the life has threads still apparent in this life. All our past lives are part of the overall memory of the soul and often weave into the present life in various ways, as memories of this life do — not because we have incomplete past lives, but because all that happens is part of our overall experience.

Out-of-body travel

As stated in Part Four, when we are asleep we all are able, as a spirit energy, to leave our bodies and travel. Whilst the spirit is away, the body is unable to move but the brain is always on alert to protect it. Therefore if there is a noise or disturbance which is unusual for the sleeping time, the brain will recall the spirit to animate the body. When this occurs, the spirit returns very quickly and can make the heart leap and palpitate.

Some spirits leave their body when it is anaesthetised as in an operation. A spirit does not have to remain in its body when it is inactive due to anaesthetic, drugs or shock. It will hover near its body and periodically return to try to activate it.

When an operation is lengthy and the body and brain are deeply anaesthetised, the spirit can travel and, on occasions, reaches a soul dimension. The brain draws it back as the anaesthetic wears off, or the spirit will be told to return to its body by a soul, as the pre-chosen dying time has not yet been reached. These experiences are well documented and sometimes called a 'return from death'. It is the spirit's need to return to its body, because it has not died, which brings it back.

On returning to consciousness the person concerned will recall being out of the body and seeing themselves unconscious, and even have a memory of being in another place which they believe to be the afterlife.

Déjà vu

It is possible for our spirit to meet another spirit whilst both bodies are asleep, hold a conversation and leave little or no memory on waking. If we meet the same person shortly afterwards, when awake, we realise we know what is going to be said next. We are, in fact, repeating the conversation our spirits have already had.

Before going to sleep, we can state where we would like our spirit to go; if it is possible, the spirit will go there. All the sights and experiences will be sent back to the brain, which will try to cover them with dreams to make them recordable. If, on waking, a note is made of all you can recall, you should be able to sort out the unusual from the mundane in the dream.

Whilst we are awake the brain records all it receives via its senses — touch, smell, hearing and taste. It does not easily record what its spirit sends back whilst it is away.

The spirit of a person can, whilst the body sleeps, go to a place, wander around and note various objects, passages or rooms. We then visit that place physically while awake and, although we have never been there physically before, we know exactly what lies around a corner, or we recognise objects or persons and are able to say correctly where rooms or staircases are.

However, if a person goes, when awake, to a place which has been altered, rearranged, or is even a ruin, and is able to say accurately how it was in the past, this is usually a sign that they knew about that place in a past life. They remember how it was from their own past life record.

Some out-of-body spirits meet the spirit energy of people known in this lifetime and who have returned to their soul through the death of their physical body.

There have been reports of people who begin to wake and find themselves paralysed, terrified, and sense a presence in the room or a force pressing down on them, or against them. Some say it is a spirit or a ghost or even an animal. It is none of these — it is their own spirit trying to enter its body on its return after the brain has become active. The spirit must return to its body if its brain awakes due to noise or disturbance, or if another spirit essence should be sensed near its body.

To stop this terrifying experience, breathe deeply and suspend thought. Thinking activates the brain and it will repel what it feels is an intruder. As soon as thinking and fear are suspended, the spirit can return simply and quietly and the body can activate again. Bodies cannot move whilst their spirit is away, because it is the spirit which animates the body.

It is possible for the spirit to travel out of its body while it is fully awake. The benefit is full memory, as the brain is active and able to receive the events sent back without the need to cover them with dreams. It accepts the impressions because they appear to come via the senses; the body cannot move whilst its spirit is away whether we are awake or asleep.

It is wise to choose a time when you will not be disturbed by things such as telephones, doorbells, shouting and other daytime noises, which the brain could translate as a threat to the body, when the spirit will immediately return. The brain can, however, cope with normal night noises without being disturbed. So it is best to do this out-of-body travel at night, or to go to a secluded place where there is no chance of disturbance.

Travelling out of your body

You need to sit in a comfortable high-backed chair with arms to hold your body upright while your spirit is out. Have by your side a buzzer set for ten minutes and a drink.

Sit in the chair and breathe deeply. Then, breathing normally, tell your spirit to leave. Fix your mind on a point across the room. If your spirit feels safe it will begin to detach. The first hurdle you may have to overcome is a feeling of nausea. You may also feel fear. These sensations will keep your spirit from leaving. Keep practising until your ten minutes are up.

Try again another time, and again, until you find you are viewing your body from the outside. Via your spirit you will see yourself sitting in the chair and will notice the light which attaches your spirit to your physical body. That light, or cord, is always there however far you go. It only fades on the death of the body.

At this point your spirit may return quickly as it realises the brain is still conscious. Remember that the brain is fully awake at this stage, and transfers its thoughts to the spirit. Accept that you are the spirit, move gently away from your body and explore the room. As a spirit you can float or walk. Take yourself to the top of cupboards and see what is there that you had forgotten. If before you start the exercise you place a coin date side up, without looking at it, on top of a cupboard, you can check the date on your return. This will enable you to prove that the experience was neither imagination nor a dream.

When you are ready to return to your body, or the buzzer has sounded, your spirit will gently slip back. Sip your drink, touch a solid object, like a table, stand up and move around. Your body may feel a little stiff.

When you repeat the exercise another time, go up to a wall and pass through it. As a spirit you cannot open doors but you can go through them. Explore the house, passing through floors, walls and doors.

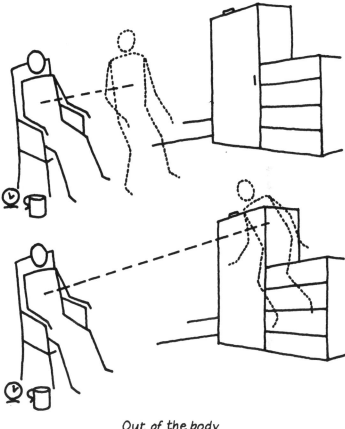

Out of the body

When you are confident in the house you can go out into the street, and travel anywhere you wish. Some of you will have a sensation of flying, others will find they are in another place in an instant. You can travel to other countries and by prearrangement meet the spirits of friends who have also left their bodies, and travel together.

Always have a drink on return, as your body dehydrates when you leave it. And always touch a solid object to establish reality in your mind.

When you feel confident, you can extend your stay-out time. Out-of-body travel while you are awake takes time and patience and not everyone can achieve it, but the total recall is worth the effort.

PART SIX

The effect of energy

We are constantly affected by our own
energy and the energy of life around us,
knowingly or not. This section explains
how we can be aware of this.

Sound and colour

Energy is transmitted and received on many levels, by all kinds of life in many ways. The energy of colour and sound can create harmony and joy or misery and terror. It depends on the state not only of the sender but also of the receiver as to how these energies are received and translated.

Music can be pleasing to one section of the community and disturbing to another. The music may be played with joy and enthusiasm but not be received in that way. Music which is soft and soothing to some is irritating and depressing to others. Certain music can affect our brain patterns. As with music, so with colour. Colours which make the wearer feel alive and happy could, when seen by someone else, cause a feeling of nausea. It is therefore important that each of us chooses what we receive and tries to think of others before transmitting into their space.

As we are all both transmitters and receivers, we need to be as careful of what we send as of what we receive. Sound is a very powerful energy, which can both build and destroy. The sounds sent out and received are very important to the well-being of all creatures. There are people who purposely create sights, sounds and scenes to cause imbalance in others.

Discordant music causes discordant thinking and even panic. Harmony builds harmonious people. Low, deep sounds put us in touch with our physical self and our link to the earth. Drumbeats are a good example of this. High, clear sounds lift our senses and enable our spirit to reach up and out for clarity and inspiration. A balance of sounds is essential to our well-being.

Every sound we produce has an effect on the atmosphere and the people who hear it. Each sound we present to the world should be carefully chosen and given with care. Once released, it can never be recalled.

A sound which affects all people is that of their own name. The energy of our name should blend and honestly represent us to others. An unrepresentative name can cause confusion and frustration.

Many people change their name for professional reasons. They believe their name is not glamorous or commercial enough or even not acceptable to the public. What they really feel is that their name misrepresents what they want people to believe. Some continue to be called by their birth name in private, as they feel more real and comfortable with that name.

A name can inspire or depress, it can cause amusement or give status. When we communicate our name to another person we should feel secure, comfortable and confident that it gives a correct and honest vibration to represent us. If a name is flat, ends abruptly or breaks in the centre, it can severely affect progress. By saying the name out loud you can ascertain the sound flow and the type of vibration from it. A psychic who has the ability can sense the correct sound and vibration for a person who needs a name change.

Some people have a vibrant personality which coupled with their energy sound can sway thousands to follow them and believe in their speeches and views, whether the content be constructive or destructive. The vibration of their voice attracts, and as more hear, more believe; and so the energy is strengthened and more are attracted. Some of the listeners will be amazed when they go away and find time to think, wondering how they became so impressed by the flow of words. Others, who have a need for a leader, will become quite fanatical and fight to stay with the person who spoke, refusing to accept criticism, defending them and sometimes alienating friends and family. It is not only the content of the speech that attracts, it is the energy of the person.

All similar objects vibrate the same. Similar birds,

animals, colours, shapes, sounds and so on will attract more of the same. 'Birds of a feather flock together' is a saying we all know, and it applies to a wide range of attractions. If a group of people are in a room together, the strongest energy will regulate the mood of the company. If the strongest energy is optimistic, the pessimists or depressives will find it hard not to smile and to agree, perhaps grudgingly, that things are not so bad. If a party is dull and boring, one person of strong, positive energy entering the room will energise the atmosphere and everyone will feel like dancing and talking. A really good party can take a dive when a strong negative person arrives; the laughter and dancing will gradually fade away.

A psychic can affect company unknowingly, but a psychic person who has control can consciously change the atmosphere of a group by building up colour energy and then extending it into the atmosphere. Colours and creative energies are very strong, and a clothes designer who has worked on a new collection in utmost secrecy can find that other design houses have chosen the same colour scheme or shape, seemingly completely at random. The picture or colour energy has become strong and intensified by all those who are sworn to secrecy. It has impressed itself on the atmosphere, where like minds will tune into the energy and think they have been inspired with a new idea, only to find it belongs to someone else.

Energy 8

Here is an exercise to increase contact and intunement with a person for healing or reading. It can also be used to increase contact for absent healing, for finding people who are lost, and to experience the essence of plants. It is called Energy 8. Use the exercise with care and discretion, and do not use it on anything you fear.

Exercise using Energy 8

When using this method on a person for a reading or healing, sit opposite them. You should send a line of energy from a point midway between yourself and the client, round the right side of the person at solar centre level, round their back to emerge at their left side, crossing over at mid-centre point, passing by your left side, round your back, emerging at the right side to join up mid-centre point. This makes a figure-of-eight shape.

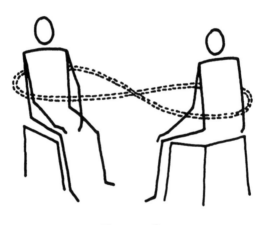

Energy 8

No more than twenty minutes should be spent on each session, and always end by cutting the Energy 8.

While doing this exercise you are sending and receiving energy. Send the colours of healing energy through the Energy 8. You may receive images, sense pain on occasion, and also receive information to help intunement. Observe the person, feel the energy flow, and translate the senses you receive.

To find a person, image them or look at a photograph of them. Send the Energy 8 round the image or photograph. You can then sense where they are or can send a thought to ask them to make contact.

You can also use Energy 8 to experience plant life. It is best to start with a tree. Sit in front of the tree you wish to experience. Send the Energy 8 around it. Feel the tree with your hands, smell it, listen to its branches and leaves whispering, taste the air around it, look at the roots, trunk, branches and leaves. Sense all these things inwardly. Close your eyes and feel the tree around you. Be the tree. You will feel well rooted, tall and flexible, firm and movable, in touch with earth and sky, in touch with your inner and outer selves. This exercise should be done in stages. Take your time — it cannot be hurried.

Whether or not you experience the essence of plants or animals, you will have a closer, deeper sense of life and being.

You will not leave your body. You will not take over the object of your exercise, and it will not take you over. You sense and feel. If you do this exercise properly, you will experience being that object but you will not be in danger.

The Energy 8 can be used for creative pursuits as well, though here there is no time limit. You will flow in accordance with your own energy pattern. If you have planned to write, collect together the paper, pen, typewriter etc. Sit quietly. Send the Energy 8 in creative green around the implements and around yourself as already explained. Begin to write or type anything you choose. You will feel inspired.

The same applies to painting, drawing, sculpture and so on. Collect the materials first. Then sit quietly and send the green Energy 8 around them and yourself. Begin to work. When you have finished, cut the Energy 8 as usual.

The Energy 8 can be used in many ways but always cut it on finishing a session. To cut the Energy 8 concentrate on the mid-point and image it being severed, either by cutting off or by fading out. If you do not cut it, you remain attached to the object or person and will continue to give and receive without restoring your reserves and to no good purpose.

Partners

Where partners are concerned, we need different types at different times in our life. Energy needs and patterns change. Our partner is our energy extension. The child seeks a safe friend, the adult a lover, the very old companionship. The friend, lover and companion can be found in one person, but it is not always so, and a feeling of isolation can be felt, which can cause a good extension to end. This could be avoided if the missing energy is looked into and attempts made to get a balance. At various times in our life the needs can change, the priorities alter. If this is not acknowledged, the partnership can falter and seem inadequate. Some people need their energy extension to be a reflection of themself, while others seek their opposite.

If partners continue to grow individually with each other, they may choose to remain together for life. Others need to change partners because they have grown in different ways and are no longer in harmony, either as reflections or opposites. Some people survive on very little energy feed-back from their partner, some require a great deal. By looking at the partner we are with, we should be able to work out who we are and what we need.

Choice

When a choice has to be made and it is difficult to come to a decision, or it is difficult to understand a person or a situation, it helps to write a letter to ourselves. By doing this, as though we were writing to an adviser, we detach from ourselves and our choices and our understanding becomes clearer. In the letter, relate the problems or dilemma and ask for assistance. Place it in an envelope and post it to yourself. When it arrives, pick it up with no thought at all. Open it, read it, and write down your reply just as you would if someone else wrote to you for help. You will find, when you re-read your answer, that you have advised yourself and clarified your choices.

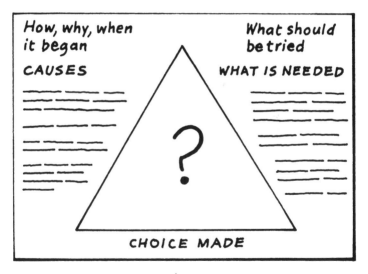

Choice

Another way to achieve clarity when you feel trapped in a situation is to draw a triangle and write down your problem in the centre. On the left side of the triangle, write down the events which led to the dilemma. Trace back to where and when the problem began. On the right side, write down what needs to be done, what help is required, who needs to be seen and what information is needed. You now have a picture of the past, the present and what can be done to help. When all possible action has been dealt with, your choice will be clearer.

You may find that the situation has improved dramatically, or that you need to remove yourself. On occasions you may find it in your own best interest to stay where you are because it suits you to do so for now. Because you have chosen to remain, you will feel in control. You are there from choice until you choose to leave.

Goal-making

Stress is caused by an imbalance in life's energy patterns. One reason for stress is striving to attain unreachable goals. If a goal is out of sight, it is hard to visualise and becomes too difficult to achieve. Small achievements give encouragement. When setting a goal, work out what is needed to achieve it. You can then plan the steps and pace your energy.

It is foolish to continue striving for a chosen goal which has become unobtainable or no longer suits. A wise person is brave enough to say: 'I have changed my mind and my goal.' A fool pushes on, unhappy and disillusioned, rather than begin something new. Never be too proud to say: 'I have changed my mind.'

All action in life can be used, whether the result is as planned or totally different. There is no waste — a purpose and meaning can be found for all that happens to us.

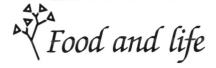

Food and life

Food is energy and the food we eat should fit the body we live in. Each physical body has its own needs. A body which is forced to eat food it finds hard to digest and change into energy will lack energy, purpose and well-being. A person who chooses a particular diet, for moral or religious reasons, should also question themselves to see if they can physically survive on what they are eating and if it really enables them to function in a healthy, alert manner.

Some bodies need vegetables only, some need fish or meat as well, some need dairy foods, some do not. The brain knows what the body needs and will try to tell the mind what is required.

All food comes from living matter which dies in order that others may live. From the most basic life form to the most developed, each lives off the other. Nature keeps balance in the world by the interaction between various life forms. The energy of plants, animals and fish remains until the physical part rots, when the value of it changes and can cause illness instead of bringing health and energy.

Eating animals, fish and fowl is not wrong in itself. The important considerations are whether the creature was allowed a full and happy life before death, and how it dies. The energy of an animal which has been factory-reared is dull, fearful and undeveloped, and it is this which affects the person eating it.

All food should be used. If something is to die, whether it be plant or animal, for another to live, every part should be used. Nothing fresh should be discarded.

Plant life which is purpose-grown will hold its freshness and therefore its life energy for longer, when picked, than wild plants. When plants which have not been purpose-grown are picked they fade and die very quickly, losing their energy as soon as they are brought into the house. Their purpose is to beautify the earth; when this purpose is removed, they fade. But plants and flowers which are grown in hothouses retain their life energy when picked and brought into houses because the indoor life seems natural to them.

All types of life react to violence, and leave that energy on the atmosphere, which we all share. Because a tree or a fish are not heard, it does not mean they do not make a noise or feel. Each section of life has its lower and higher sensitivity levels. Just as some humans have a high, and some have a low, threshold to pain, so too do fish, animal, bird and plant life.

Whatever we eat, it is the energy of that food which helps us to live. So it follows that we should choose with care how our food is grown, obtained and made available for eating, whatever it is.

Ghosts, spirits, essence and poltergeists

These energies are different, but are constantly confused with each other.

Ghosts

Ghosts are energy images left on the atmosphere by intense emotion or fear. When a person dies in horrific or dramatic circumstances, the energy of the event is left at the place of the experience. The spirit is not present. There is no mind or thought process. A ghost cannot alter its actions or route. It is an impression. A ghost cannot hurt or interfere with life in any way. If you stood in the path of a moving ghost image, it would go past you or through you. You may feel a nervous quiver, but that is your own fear. The energy impressions of what we do record all the time, but if they are not seen and thereby energised they gradually fade away. Human energy changes the atmosphere and the ghostly image becomes stronger and lasts longer. Some ghosts have been seen for centuries because they have become well known and people make a point of observing them, thus constantly recharging the atmosphere.

The ghost of Anne Boleyn was seen to walk on the ramparts of the Tower of London. As she walked to her death by decapitation, the horror of her situation would have been very acute. She would have realised there was no escape, no reprieve, and each step she took toward her executioner had to be measured and calm. The self-control needed to suppress the horror would have been very intense. The impression was imprinted very sharply on the atmosphere and stones of the building, and after her death she was seen walking in the same place.

Whenever ghostly images are seen, they attract. People gather, hoping to get a glimpse of the ghost. Their fear and excitement create a strong energy and charge the atmosphere, making the ghost more visible. As time passes and fewer people gather, the image will begin to fade.

Ghosts of headless horsemen are well known and well documented. When horses were our only means of transport, messengers would gallop miles to deliver letters or get help. One way to halt your enemy's messenger was to stretch twine across the road. The twine was carefully placed to unseat the rider, but on occasions would decapitate him. The horse would gallop on with the rider, minus head, still seated. The intensity of the energy of the event left an impression of a headless horseman who gallops in a certain place and disappears.

If a house is built where a ghost is seen, the ghost will be seen in the house. Remember, a ghost cannot move from its place. It is an impression. It has no will, no mind and is harmless. The less it is looked at, the less it is seen, until it fades away completely.

Ghosts can occur from intensely beautiful moments, too. A picture of a meeting between people after a long separation can also be seen after the event. These images are rarely energised and so they fade quickly. Humans react very intensely to an image which frightens them, but not so to an image of delight.

Some ghosts look and feel very calm and beautiful. They are seen walking in gardens or in a part of a house they were intensely fond of. They are welcomed by some people as attractions to their house.

Spirits

When a body dies the spirit survives, is met and returns to its soul. On very rare occasions a spirit can refuse to leave the earth after the body dies. It cannot be removed by force if it chooses to remain, but can be helped to return to its soul. These spirits can be seen and felt and are often confused with ghosts, although they are totally different in substance and behaviour. Spirits who remain have consciousness, can move at will and do not fade with time. They stay for a variety of reasons: refusal to accept the fact that their body is dead; strong ties to property, money or a person; a love of a particular place; a sense of injustice at their treatment in life, and so on.

Spirits who have stayed on earth for a possessive reason or out of a sense of injustice can cause noises to be heard, lights to switch on and off, furniture to move, and doors to open and shut. On their own they cannot move anything physical as they have no physical energy, but if a living person is present the spirit can use that person's energy to make physical things move. Most spirit activity occurs late in the evening or at night, when most people are at home resting or sleeping and their energy is available for the spirit to use.

No spirit belongs on earth after the death of the body, whether it be beautiful and harmless or bitter and harmful. A psychic who is able can help spirits to leave and return to their soul where they came from. A spirit cannot progress whilst it remains on earth.

Visiting a medium and receiving a message from the spirit of a person who has died is totally different; that spirit is not based on earth, but with its soul. They connect for a specific reason and do not hold the connection longer than necessary — usually only minutes, and rarely more than once.

Most spirits who refuse to leave stay only a very short time. They feel the energy of their soul recalling them and soon grow weary of their lonely existence. When this happens, their spirit helpers show them the way to their soul home and friends.

 Helping a spirit energy to depart

Persuading a determined spirit to leave takes patience, understanding and, on occasion, strong nerves. Do not attempt it unless you are sure you can see it through to their departure. If you are afraid, the spirit will use the energy of that fear to frighten you away.

Do not have a companion with you unless he or she is also psychic, and make sure your companion can cope with any occurrence. Your whole attention must be on the spirit. You cannot be worrying about anyone else.

Spirits can move around, although some guard a particular place. Walk round the house until you sense or see them. Sit quietly, and ask in your mind for help. This is very important, as the soul energies will help you and when the spirit is ready to leave, will show them the way.

Ascertain why the spirit refuses to leave. Reason with it. Explain that it no longer belongs here. In most cases the spirit will be reasonable, and pleased to have someone with whom it can communicate. If there is something it wishes done or a message it wishes to pass on, you can, if possible, carry out those wishes. When it is satisfied and agrees to leave, the spirit helpers will take over and they will all leave together.

Once a spirit has agreed to leave, it cannot return. Spirits rarely remain on earth very long after the body dies. Their attachments to earth matters fade very quickly.

It has been known for spirits to try to frighten people. They have also been known to create bad smells, and even to cause objects to fly through the air. Some of the objects will not be real, although they appear quite solid. But some objects are real and you may have to move sharply to avoid them. Remember, they are using your energy to do this.

 ## Clearing ceremony

When the spirit has left, clear the room as follows.

You will need flowers for each room, a candle and free-running salt. Place some flowers in the middle of the room, and light the candle. Go to the doorway and walk round the room in a clockwise direction, scattering the salt very lightly, until you reach the door again. Pick up the candle and go out of the room. Shut the door. Sprinkle the salt along the base of the door outside.

Now perform the same ceremony in every room in the house, starting at the room furthest from the front door. All rooms, landings and staircases should be treated in the same way. The front door is done last. Go outside and sprinkle salt along the foot of the front door.

The house is now clear, cleaned and ready to be used by living occupants. This ceremony is also used to clear a house when moving home and to neutralise a ley energy line in a house.

Essence

Most reports of paranormal activity are caused by humans and their energy. In this instance I call the energy 'essence'. It can be mistaken for ghosts and/or spirits, but is neither. It is this essence that horror stories are based on. In its negative state it can be very frightening, but in its positive state it feels very beautiful. Humans affect the atmosphere, making it positive or negative.

Negative essence

If a person in a deeply depressive state sits in a public place brooding about killing themselves, whether they carry this out or not they will leave on the atmosphere an energy pattern of despair which can remain for hours, only gradually fading away. Should another person sit in the same spot before the energy pattern has cleared, they too can begin to feel depressed and low in energy. When they leave, the energy in the area will be stronger still. The more people who sit there, the stronger the energy pattern will become, until it begins to attract depressed people.

Eventually someone will succeed in killing themselves there, and then others will follow and the place will become known as a bad spot. Some places are well known for suicide attempts due to their build-up of negative energy patterns.

A place where a murder has occurred will vibrate strongly with the fear and horror of the event. Even people who did not know of the murder will sense the fear and become uneasy and frightened, adding to the energy pattern.

When a traumatic car accident occurs, the energy pattern will be impressed on the road. Should other car drivers go through that spot soon afterwards, they may feel uneasy or out of control and soon another accident will occur, then another. The place then gets labelled as an accident black-spot. Some drivers will report seeing a blackness or a white shape appearing in front of them before they crashed. This is a build up of an energy pattern. If a person lives in a house where they are very unhappy, that sad energy pattern can be impressed on the house. Other people will feel sad when they visit.

A person who has been very cruel and sadistic to people in a house will impress that energy pattern on it. This will be felt by visitors, who will want to leave but not know why. If someone with a weak character visits, this person can link into the energy pattern and behave very cruelly, either by word or by deed. Sometimes their behaviour seems totally out of character. The longer they stay, the more they will pick up and retain, and will find it hard to return to their known character on leaving.

A house which has a history of cruelty, pain, despair or murder attached to it can become an attraction to sensation seekers. Their negative excitement and fear vibrations will add to the essence already present.

Some houses get a reputation for being haunted. It is not necessarily a ghost or spirit, however, but this human energy pattern essence building up until it is felt like a presence. This make people feel nervous and frightened and some, feeling the vibration, will imagine what it is. This picture then becomes part of the essence. Usually the picture is horrific, as fear of what they feel brings to their mind old horror stories or monstrous images.

Those who can sense energies will not only feel the energy but also see it, as the imagined shape put on by someone else. This explains sightings of horrendous figures dragging their partly severed limbs and weighted down by chains, skeletons in monks' robes and so on. The imagination is excellent at summoning up fearful images.

Sometimes animals are imagined and seen in various guises.

This essence can move about in a house if humans are present, as it attaches to them, but it is usually based in one room. As it comes from humans it can attach to humans. The fear that a person feels adds to it. Feeling that there is 'something' in the room with you looking over your shoulder, and catching sight of the image, are very traumatic experiences.

To remove essence in its negative form, human energy is needed in its positive form. Gather together a band of people, music, flowers and good lighting. Go to the house or room which is affected and open windows and doors. Music, singing, dancing, laughter and joy will gradually neutralise the negative energy. It may take one or many visits in this positive mood to achieve clearance, depending on the intensity of the energy to be neutralised.

Do not take anyone who is nervous or afraid. The essence can be felt and seen by some, which can be frightening. It can cause articles to move or persons to feel pushed. It is important to remember that whatever is seen is the result of someone's imagination; whatever is felt is an energy build-up and fear makes the vibration stronger. The party must continue irrespective of any disturbance, sightings or movements. No one should sleep whilst this clearance is being carried out. The energy of a sleeping person can add to the essence, as the person is not consciously being positive. No alcohol should be drunk, as it lessens control of the imagination and distorts human energy.

Positive essence

Positive vibrations released by people during intensely moving, emotional and deeply beautiful experiences will also impress an energy pattern on the atmosphere, which will build up as more people contribute.

Places where people are happy help lift the depression and sadness in others. Some areas are very popular, because everyone feels good when they are there. They add to the positive feeling, and it grows. They say: 'There's a wonderful atmosphere in this place.' They have helped to put it there. If a happy, contented person sits admiring the beautiful scenery or sunset, and this is followed by an unhappy person doing the same, that person can feel lifted and wonder why they worried so much.

Houses and rooms can feel warm, welcoming and secure because the people who live in them feel that way. This essence is a beautiful experience. People with a vivid imagination can put a picture of someone beautiful on the essence they feel and say it is all due to a wonderful spirit being present. People who are, or have been, deeply religious can be instrumental in shrines being created from a physical energy build-up.

This type of shrine can occur at a ley energy site. When ley energies cross, the area becomes charged and the glow can be seen above the ground. It hovers and gently shimmers, giving an impression of life and mobility. The shapes vary in size according to the ley energy, but they are usually six feet or more in height and can hover any height above the ground, twelve feet or even more. The energy is usually white or blue, although in some areas the atmospheric conditions can cause it to look yellow, red or green. This type of ley energy can be seen by sensitive people or those with uncluttered minds. Children see them very clearly because their minds are able to accept, wonder and fantasise more easily than those of adults.

When young people whose background is simple or religious, for example, see this glowing shape, they easily imagine it to be a vision of a holy person. They will honestly believe they are seeing a favourite saint appearing before them and impress this image on the energy. They stand transfixed, completely overawed, and gradually become convinced they have been chosen for a special purpose. They even believe that messages are being given to them. Afterwards they tell everyone who it was they believe they saw.

Some listeners, if they are quick and sensitive enough, will see the shimmering shape and confirm the children's story. They too will see it as the person the children said it was, and their energy will add to the atmosphere. Some of those who cannot see will say they can, so as not to be thought less devout than their neighbours.

Later, when the image fades and there is nothing to see, the story will be believed by some because those concerned are so convincing. Others will reserve opinion, hoping 'the vision' will return to prove the story.

The site will be constantly watched and the children will visit regularly. Prayers will be said, and intense feelings of wanting it to be true will all create an energy which will charge the atmosphere. People will begin to feel much better after being at the spot. A statue may be placed there. The children and/or others will eventually see the vision again, which will be when the ley energy is sufficiently charged again to rise above the ground. It will be seen as the figure the children originally claimed it to be. The intense energy created will build up those who are weak and cures will be claimed.

The site is often dug out to make a grotto, and candles and statues are placed in it. This digging usually leads to underground water being discovered. When drunk, these waters are found to be very beneficial. Those who have walking and other disabilities say they have received strength or even walked again after drinking the water. The energy which is making them well and mobile is from the people linking into the ley energy.

But there is a sad side to this kind of essence build-up: the sick persons do not always continue to feel well when they leave the shrine. Once the energy, the people and the excitement are no longer there, these people can relapse into their original state. Unless the cause of illness or disability has been removed, it will return. Yet those who find they can walk at the grotto but cannot walk on returning home should not despair: they have shown that they can walk, and could do so again if the cause of the problem is found.

If interest wanes in a particular site, the human energy will lessen. The believers who still visit benefit from the energies which will be gentle, soothing and healing, the massive human input of joy, fear, curiosity and disappointment slowly balancing with the natural earth energy.

In ancient times a magnetic stone or stones would have been placed at the site where the ley energy had been observed, and the energy used for healing.

Poltergeists

The word poltergeist means 'noisy ghost.' It is an energy based in the solar centre released by children during puberty. Usually the energy is used and absorbed by the children as they come to terms with the changes in their physical and mental being.

But some children do not utilise the energy and it builds up in strength in the solar centre, linking in with their subconscious while they sleep. The subconscious desires, resentments and oppressions, real or imagined, can then manifest and cause very physical activity to occur.

The energy of a child who blames a particular person for injustice, imagined or not, can cause furniture to move, beds to shake and covers to be pulled off that sleeping person. Their favourite china will be smashed, pictures ruined and wallpaper ripped; cans of paint may explode and their contents shoot up the walls and over ceilings.

The child will be asleep when all this occurs and is not a suspect. Some children activate the energy through a subconscious need for attention, due to too little physical and mental activity. The cause should be sought and the children given the opportunity to speak about their needs and resentments. Changes should then be made, if necessary, and understanding achieved.

Golden lights

Many psychics perceive lights passing on the periphery of their vision when they are involved in an activity which uses the mind. These lights are usually a golden colour but are sometimes seen as white, blue or green. The size can be as small as a pinhead or as large as a snowflake. They move in groups and are not visible with the physical eyes.

These lights are not to be confused with floaters, which is an optical condition, or spots before the eyes, which is a medical condition. They are totally different. The golden lights are always at the side of the vision, and to appreciate them it is essential that the mind and imagination are controlled. If you see them, continue with what you are doing, but in your mind say: 'If possible, please show yourself.'

These lights are spirit energy. They each represent a spirit which is moving through the atmosphere for a specific purpose and psychics can see them. Sometimes they will float by and disappear. On occasions, however, they pause and, using our energy, can gradually build up into a face. We can, on occasions, converse with them in our mind. They will fade in due course.

Thought forming

This is a method of using the energy of thinking to enable certain changes. The art of thought forming is to be precise. It is advisable not to thought form for things which belong to other people (someone else's job, partner, home, possessions, and so on). If you do, it can have very unpleasant repercussions for you. You will have attracted something or someone away from their own framework, probably without their knowledge, and interfered with their plans. The person or whatever you have attracted will eventually return to their original plan and you will be the loser. A strong person will not be affected by a thought form. It is also inadvisable to thought form for sums of money, as you may lose in order to gain. Absent healing is an acceptable thought form: we send out with the purpose of sharing healing energy, and the thought behind it is of health and well-being for the receiver.

 ## How to thought form purposefully

Write down exactly what you need, or draw it in a series of pictures. Read what you have written or look at your drawing intently, gaze at the space in front of you and impress the image on the air. Then forget it. Do not think about it for twenty-four hours, then repeat the exercise at the same time in the same way.

Example 1: For a person who has a shop and needs more customers, picture the shop door with 'Open' on it. Picture people walking in the door, picking up some goods, buying them and walking out of the shop looking very happy. Repeat every twenty-four hours.

Example 2: For a person finding it difficult to sell their house, picture the house with a large 'Sold' notice in front of it and a cheque for the asking price in the hand of the seller. Repeat every twenty-four hours.

Example 3: Before a job interview, picture yourself at the interview. See yourself feeling confident, being offered the job and holding the confirmation letter in your hand. Repeat every twenty-four hours.

If a project is held up for want of money, do not picture money, but picture the completed project and smiling faces at the achievement. Repeat every twenty-four hours.

Back up the thought form with normal procedures. The house for sale has to be put on the market; the job needs to be applied for, efforts made to get the project started and so on.

We transmit thought forms unknowingly at times, and then wonder at what we attract. Some people are lonely and feel they always meet the wrong type of person and get hurt. These people could be sending out unclear and insecure thought energy and attracting more in return. If you are uncertain about yourself and your needs, you will attract uncertainty. Check what you need. If it is a companion, compile a list of the characteristics you would like them to have. Then write next to this list what you have to offer in return. This ensures that you do not ask for more than you are able to give. When you are sure of what you are asking, prefix your list with: 'I need to meet a man/woman whose nature is . . .' and finish with the word 'today'. Repeat every twenty-four hours.

Chanting

Chanting is very intensive, and great care should be taken to be specific when using this energy. The chant must have a rhythm to it, for instance: 'Today's the day I sell my house.' Chants should be repeated twenty-five times in order to be effective. Keeping twenty-five beads on a string and moving each one along as you repeat the chant helps to keep the rhythm going without losing the count. 'Today' is definite, and it can be put into the chant even if it is impossible for the request to happen in a day. The chant can be repeated silently or out loud and no special time of day is required.

The chanting method is also used for affirmation. For instance, 'Every day I get better and better,' repeated twenty-five times, can bring about a change in health. 'Today's the day I take charge of my life,' is another beneficial affirmation. The chant method helps bring about a feeling of well-being and positive thinking. A chant can be repeated for courage: 'I have courage today to face my boss' when a confrontation is needed. 'Today I will dissolve my fears' is another.

Do not chant for money! Chant, instead, for the completion of the project, not the money to complete it. For example: 'Today I get £2,000,000' is incorrect. It is better to chant: 'Today my project reaches completion', or 'The house I need I can afford.'

And do not chant to steal! Chanting for another person's job, partner or possession is stealing, and as with thought forming for the wrong reason, will rebound on you. What you will receive will be out of its own space and will return eventually. This can cause a great deal of upset, worry and trauma to others, quite apart from yourself.

Psychokinesis

Psychokinesis is the production of motion in inanimate and far away objects by the use of psychic energy. It is possible to make inanimate objects move without touching them, and this ability works strongest when the psychic is in a state of excitement or anger. By directing energy on to the object they want to move, it can do so. Some psychics are unaware of this energy and can be frightened when it causes doors to bang, lights to turn on and off, or light bulbs to explode. On occasions the energy can move about a room in a ball or flat square shape, and it seems that an entity is present and causing the disturbance.

If this happens to you, you should remember it is your own energy and not be afraid. Sit down and become calm. If people or animals are present, the energy can be transferred to them, via the hands, beneficially. Clear the aura and, if possible, have a warm shower. Check to ascertain what caused the energy build-up, and deal with it.

This is the energy which is used to make spoons bend and metal objects twist. It can make a non-working mechanical object activate. You will find that the majority of psychics who activate this energy are in an excitable mood, talking rapidly and moving about. They can affect objects held by others even many miles away if the person is concentrating mentally, either in the same room or via TV or telephone. When this happens it appears that the other person can affect objects. When the psychic is no longer in contact, the ability ceases – unless, of course, the person is also psychic, in which case it will continue.

In daily life, this energy may be a hindrance. Electric kettles, irons, tape recorders and so on can all cut out when the psychic is near them and agitated in any way. It can cause ticket machines to reject magnetic tickets when we are hurrying to catch a train. Cars will cough and splutter if we try to start them in a hurry. If this happens, remove the key, get out of the car and calm down. On returning to the car, it will start with no trouble.

Ley line energy

All living things have energy flowing through and around them. The earth is no exception. Its energy patterns, as mentioned earlier, are known as ley lines.

Ley lines are not always straight, although there are a great many which are. The energy can spiral, zig-zag or curve. It can be deep in the earth, near or on the surface, and on occasions it can spiral above the earth's surface. It can be several feet wide.

Ancient settlements used psychics who were able, via their feet or with dowsing rods, to sense the ley energy lines whilst other people marked them with stones. When a site was found which had crossing ley lines with very strong energy making a star shape, large upright stones were placed in a ring, one on each line as it came towards the star centre. Sometimes a large monolith was placed in the centre of the star. Some of these stone circles are still in existence, and Stonehenge is perhaps the best known.

By embedding magnetic stones in the energy, the circle became usable: the ring of magnetic stones stored the energy released. The chief mystic and his initiates — people who were well versed in the ancient history and wisdom of the planet and knew how to release the energy — were able to use it for healing, fertility, harmony and the general well-being of the earth and its people. Ceremonies and special rites were performed when the energies were at a particular strength or at the change of the seasons.

After using the ley line energy circle, it was the custom for the participants to encircle it and move in a clockwise direction, slowly at first, then gradually increasing speed in order to create an energy which was absorbed by the stones and fed the ley energy. The stones acted as a battery for the energy, constantly being used and recharged by the earth and the people. Some of the ceremonies were carried out at night to harmonise and use the moon's energy.

When the original mystics and wise ones used the circles, only positive energies were used and tuned into through certain chants and movements. Contact with the earth and planet energies was their purpose.

The stones used in the ley energy circles still hold energy. If you find a complete ring of stones, or a monolith, sit near to the stone and touch it to experience the wonderful earth energies still flowing and usable.

In later times ley lines were marked by stones wherever people settled, in order to make sure no building was erected on them, and they were available for energy use. A building interferes with the energy flow. Whatever happens on a ley line is recorded in it. If the ley energy is dry, any action will only affect the part it occurred on. If, however, it is a water ley line, one which has a stream running through it, above or under the earth, the energy will flow along the line, affecting all buildings or people on it. Villages and cities used to be built alongside ley line systems so the energies could flow freely, bene-fiting all those living nearby. Settlements were built to fit the energy and so were circular, crescent- or star-shaped.

Many forts were built on ley lines, the known energy being used to build up the fighting force of the army. The defenders of the country would find the hill or mountain which was known to contain ley energy and build their fort or castle on the top, sometimes incorporating the central monolith into the building. When invaders came, the stone circles and ley line markers were protected and hidden if possible. It was known that whoever used the ley energy would be strong and powerful and the ley places were highly prized in any battle.

Where ley energy spiralled up and out in a cone spiral, earth would be used to cover or surround it. A monolith would be placed on the top to seal the energy. People could then climb up the man-made hill in a clockwise spiral, benefiting from the energy, until they reached the top where some experienced healing or felt enlightened. Others experienced visions and deep insights. Many of these mounds are still in existence. Some have a path cut into them spiralling round to benefit the climbers of the ley spiral.

We now live in a time when a number of people, whatever their beliefs, are again appreciating the needs of the earth and trying to care for the ley lines, the land, the air and the sea. They monitor the use of the earth's resources and believe that what is taken must be given back to ensure the harmony and balance of all things.

Neutralising ley energy

As ley lines can cover many miles it is very difficult to find the source of the troubled energy, but it is possible to neutralise the line where it is known to be affecting people. To do this you need a pendulum, a map of the area of the house and its surroundings, some copper wire and a hammer.

Place the map in front of you and, holding your pendulum, ask inwardly for ley energy. The pendulum will sway in the direction of the ley line. Draw a line the way the pendulum swings. Move along the map, repeating the question continuously. Some leys will be straight, others spiral. When you have drawn in all the leys in the area you should return the pendulum to the first one found and ask if water is present. If it is, the pendulum will move. Draw in a wavy line to show this. Repeat over each line. Some areas will have no ley lines, others only dry ones. Yet others will have dry and water ley energy.

Where a ley line goes through a house, treat all the rooms as follows. Hammer a half inch of copper wire into the floor in every corner of the room, whether it be an inside or outside corner. Go outside the house and put more copper wire at every corner of the house. Push the copper wire in the earth or concrete so that it touches the building. If your house is attached to another and your neighbour does not want his or her house touched use the line that joins the two houses as your corner.

When the house has been copper-wired inside and out, perform the clearing ceremony (see p. 152), ending by walking around the house, if you can, in a clockwise direction, sprinkling salt.

The house is now neutralised, and only events which occur in your own household will affect the ley energy.

Some people tack the copper wire all round the rooms and all round the outside of the house, but this is not really necessary. It is the corners that are all-important.

The effects of the ceremony can be noticed very soon. The house will feel clean, clear and light. When the negative event occurred further away and has been carried by the water to affect the area, the copper and salt ceremonies will clear, clean and lighten the house and neutralise the ley line, so that all houses on the ley flow will also be cleared.

Tree energy

Plant life has an aura and emits energy. Certain flowers and plants are very attractive to us and we feel uplifted when we are near them; all our senses activate. All forms of plant life are used to make medicines, creams, potions and so on. Trees supply air, shelter, warmth, food and comfort to many living creatures, including ourselves. They are held sacred in various beliefs.

The energy of trees affects humans in many ways. When there are many of them together, towering above us, as in a forest, we can feel intimidated and frightened. Others, gently swaying in the summer breeze, fill us with delight.

Many people have a great affection for an individual tree, turning to it for comfort when they are lonely or sad. They feel the tree's energy and are uplifted. Various trees have quite noticeable effects on certain people and I give some examples below. I have found that standing near a tree, placing both hands on the trunk or even embracing the tree (where appropriate), enables the energy to be experienced.

Oak:
Strength of purpose is given by an oak tree. It will also remove headaches and indecision.

Willow:
Lifts depression and helps aspiration.

Plane:
Encourages straight, clear thinking and logic.

Mountain ash or rowan:
For spiritual energy and intunement with the inner self.

Birch:
For removal of negative and destructive thought, and for action.

Cedar:
For inner peace and serenity.

Chestnut:
For laughter, removes pomposity.

Yew:
Removes fear and paranoia.

Lignum vitae:
Gives energy to the physical and a feeling of belonging. Very good for those who have lost touch with reality.

Beech:
Helps the lonely and lost.

De-labelling

All people react to the energy of labels, whether their own or those on others. We put them on people and on ourselves and perform accordingly.

Labels are an integral part of life and enable us to identify and react in various situations. In every group of people there is a leader and there are followers, a weak person, a strong one, a bully, a victim, a gentle person and so on. It begins in families and follows through school, work, communities, towns, countries, continents. When labels become obstacles to natural and spontaneous living, they cause guilt, fear, emotional instability and physical pain. When 'reading' a person, you may be able to sense if it is a label which is causing the trouble. Many people have problems with parent labels. This works both ways – parents using their label to manipulate their offspring and offspring allowing the parents to do this by their reaction.

There is no natural reason why we should like our

parents or they should like us. Respect and love are earned by our behaviour. Some adults, perhaps parents themselves, become children when they visit their own parents, allowing them to behave in an autocratic manner, to undermine confidence and to insist on certain duties being performed. They use their parent label as a power tool, and the adult child allows them to do so. The adult offspring feel guilty when they resent their parents' behaviour, accepting it because they did when they were children and it is a habit to accept and not question. They cannot confront the parent because they are afraid, just as they were as a child, of the resulting temper or deep hurt that the parent uses as a weapon. They visit their parents from a sense of duty, and each visit is demoralising, exhausting and dreaded.

Take off the label of 'parent' and 'child' and replace it with the label 'adults'. Each is a person entitled to their own personality but not entitled to inflict it on another person. Once we see our parents as people we will be in control of our feelings and actions and not go into a robotic state. We will be able to understand them better and why they behave as they do. By understanding another person's strengths and weaknesses, we can adjust accordingly. They no longer have the power the parent label gave them.

We can choose to visit them because we can cope with who they are. We may not choose them as friends, but we know them and can show care. We may find they refuse help or we do not want to be involved with them. We may choose to keep an eye on them and be ready to help when needed because they are fellow beings, not because we feel guilty or duty bound.

Some people use the parent label to project personal ambitions on to their children. They decide when the children are young that they will take up a certain profession. They push them through school and constantly remind them of the goals they have to achieve. When the grown child fails the exams, or rebels and takes up a totally different type of life, these parents feel let down and complain that their time and money have been wasted, the child has failed, missed his or her potential and is ungrateful. The offspring's friends are blamed for leading him or her from the chosen path.

We are all born with potential, but it is our own potential. Each of us needs stimulation, knowledge, encouragement, but towards our own goals, not someone else's. Parents should check their behaviour and motivation during the years their children are growing up to make sure they are not inflicting their own lost chances on to their offspring, that they do not expect, but accept the child in their care and encourage it to be what it is, not what the parent thinks it should be. This also applies to loved ones – allow them their own level of growth, and do not push them to be what you think they are capable of.

Offspring should, as soon as they become knowledgeable, look at their parents and see them as people. Before the parent label was attached to them, they were ordinary human beings, living life their own way, within their own boundaries. Becoming a parent does not mean acquiring instant wisdom, or that love and understanding are instantly available. If people are inadequate before parenthood, they will be inadequate afterwards. Do not expect parents to be what they are not. Allow them to be people. We all make mistakes, but with the parent/child label system this human non-perfect behaviour is shied away from, hidden and covered up, each side expecting more than there is, each believing they have the right to expect certain reactions because of the roles they are playing. This can result in emotional blackmail.

Roles can be reversed at any time. Labels change and can be changed by investigating how we behave wearing a certain label. By refusing to use labels of power to manipulate, and encouraging others to be responsible for themselves, we will find the label system works very well — in other words, when it is not used to cause fear, pain and guilt, or for power trips.

If, when 'reading', you sense that the person is suffering guilt from the label system, you can help that person to face their guilt and remove it by sensing the person behind the label which is causing the distress, whether it be the person sitting in front of you or someone else.

We should all be responsible for our own behaviour, whether it be as parent or offspring, employer or employee, teacher or pupil, cared for or caring, and so on. And we should all exercise the right to choose our friends and the right to remove ourselves from the presence of any person who is using a label to manipulate us.

Personal assessment

Assessment means updating who we are so that we are living in the present with clarity and control. We have a tendency to forget that we have learned and grown through experience. We can still behave and think as we were, perhaps, years previously.

If we still behave as a junior at work, for instance, we will be treated as one. If we still behave as a small child when with our parents, they will treat us as one. If we are unreliable, we will be let down. If we are unhappy about how we are being treated, we can assess ourself to see if it is what we are projecting.

It takes honesty and courage to write an assessment of yourself. Put the heading down first: How do I see myself as a friend, sibling, offspring, parent, employee etc. Write how you behave. See if you are still behaving and thinking as you did years previously. You may find that complaints about your treatment by others are due to your own behaviour.

 Day plan

Some people are unable to cope with life because they feel they have too much to do in too short a time, with too little energy. These people will be helped by what I call the SOS system:

Self 8 *hours*							
Others 8 *hours*							
Serenity 8 *hours*							

By keeping a check on what each hour is really used for and marking it on the chart each day, it is possible to see just how the time is used. 'Self' covers all activity we are involved in which is mainly for ourselves, such as bathing, eating, leisure and meditation. 'Others' covers activities including work, voluntary services, and cleaning the home, if that is your job. 'Serenity' covers the hours in which we sleep or rest.

Each section has eight hours and hours can be borrowed from another section, but must be paid back. Here is an example. At the end of day one, if ten hours have been used on work, the two extra hours were borrowed from 'Self' time and must be paid back. During day two eight hours were worked, eight hours were used for 'Self' and eight hours for sleep. Nothing owing. On day three you overslept one hour, so one hour is owed to 'Self'; you worked nine hours, so one hour is owed to 'Self'; and you slept eight hours. Two hours are now owed to 'Self' plus another two hours from day one.

Add up the hours each day through the week, remembering that lunch and tea breaks, travel time and personal chatting are all 'Self' time and cannot be counted as work. All naps and dozes are 'Serenity' time, and only work done is counted as work — not time spent at a workplace. You will be very suprised at where your time has been spent. If you find you owe yourself eight hours, have a day off work (if you can) to recoup them. If you find you spend too much time on yourself during worktime, stay late and get your work up-to-date.

The above method can be used in many ways. It is excellent for helping people see their space and plan guilt- and resentment-free days.

Negative energy and 'possession'

Possession means that someone or something is in control of another's brain and body — a spirit, other than their own, is residing in their body and has taken complete control. Cases of possession have not been proved. A spirit essence does not leave its soul until a planned new life on earth is prepared.

To believe in possession presupposes that there are malevolent spirits which are unattached to a soul, or to a human in a physical state. But most so-called possession cases are negative energy attachments, not spirit attachment.

People who have negative energy around them can

frighten their family, friends and themselves by their mood swings and behaviour. Some are taken, or go, to exorcists who put them through a ritual which usually mentions devils and evil spirits. The classic belief in ritual, incense, chanting and the power in objects to remove possessing spirits is based on fear — mainly the fear of the exorcist and the observers. Any fear around the person will add to the negative energy.

An object will only have meaning if the person believes in it. The object has only the energy put into it; it has none of its own. The person in distress becomes more and more frightened by the words, the exorcist's behaviour and the atmosphere and can even experience a fit or convulsion caused through fear and stress. This is believed to mean that a devil or entity is leaving, and the exorcism is claimed to be successful. However, the exorcised person can be physically and mentally disturbed more by this experience than by the negative energy which was causing the confusion originally. An aura clean, healing energy transference, counselling and changes in lifestyle are what are needed to clear the negative energy in the aura. This will also clear the mind and the brain, enabling the person to feel clear, spiritually strong and in control again.

A negative energy build-up can occur around a person who is using their own energy unwisely, or where people gather and fear is present. From the vibration caused by the fears and terrors of these people negative energy grows and circulates, attaching to the weakest people in the company. These people can take with them, in their aura, the negativity, fear and impressions of those around them, and through that negative energy relive the fears and torments of the people who released it. Combined with their own imagination and terror, the result can appear very like a possession. A change in character and erratic behaviour, alternating between sense and nonsense, can occur. This is not possession, but a negative energy build-up combined with fear.

Some people with mental imbalance, disturbed personalities or psychiatric disorders have negative energy in their aura. These symptoms could be helped by having this negative energy build-up removed.

We all have many facets to our character, and because a person changes it does not mean that they are possessed or have a negative aura energy. If the different sides of our character are not allowed to grow, to be seen and a choice of behaviour made and experienced, a person will live a false life. The outward impression may be one of calm, control, kindness and understanding, while inside hatred, stress and resentment boil away.

These suppressed people can change character in certain circumstances or conditions, allowing the hidden side to manifest. They sometimes only show this side to one person, usually a partner or child. This is not possession; these people need counselling, healing and understanding.

PART SEVEN

The soul,
the spirit and
physical existence

I realise that some of the subject matter in this book is different, and may seem strange to those readers who have learnt other ways of looking at psychics and what they can do.

The following section, covering the existence of the soul and spirit, may also seem new and therefore different. However, the concept given is believed and accepted by many spiritually aware people, including, of course, myself. It is included in the interest of sharing knowledge with open-minded seekers.

The soul, the spirit and physical existence

Our souls have free will and self responsibility. They have a choice how they exist and progress. When the soul is ready it chooses to experience a life on earth via its spirit energy. The soul does not come to earth.

The soul's friends and advisers help to assess reasons and select the most suitable parents, situation and location. The soul also chooses the time of leaving when our physical body dies to release the spirit.

With help and understanding, the soul builds up a picture of what its spirit energy could achieve while on earth. This is not pre-programming. The spirit energy, working through its physical body inheritance, has to make its own choices whilst on earth.

Birth

The soul does not leave its level of evolution. It is the complete consciousness and has a record of all its life experiences on earth and its continuous evolution as a soul. The spirit is the energy of, and a reflection of, the soul which connects with the pregnant woman at conception, becoming acclimatised to the new life environment and the constrictions of earth life. At the twelfth week of pregnancy, the spirit enters and receives all its energy from the foetus, which is usually sensed as a movement or quiver at this time, and is known as the 'quickening'. Until that connection the energy of the mother has supported the spirit. The spirit can then enter and leave the unborn child at will, but is joined at all times by the spirit energy cord which will remain attached to the physical body until the dying day is reached.

On the day of birth the spirit decides if it wishes to be

born with the physical body or observe the birth. Birth does not need to be experienced by the spirit; although its energy is needed to boost the physical effort, this assistance can be given from outside the body.

Life

At the moment of birth the memory of our previous soul existence begins to fade. To remember the greatness of our soul and all it has learned, achieved and experienced would make earth life unbearable and unlivable, as the spirit is restricted by the physical energies which surround it.

As physical beings we attract opportunities. Some people attract many opportunities near to each other. The opportunities we need occur as we proceed, whichever path we follow or however many times we alter during our stay here. It is how the opportunity is dealt with which gives it purpose, not the opportunity itself — we have free will regarding how we live and how we choose to behave. Things we do or do not do affect other people and their growth, whether planned or not.

When we are in our infancy, our parents/guardians are responsible for our well-being. They are also responsible for what we see, hear, smell, touch and taste. Young humans learn by copying what is around them, and their first seven years are the main observing and learning times. The brain is busy recording all its experiences. Parents, guardians and teachers are responsible for our education, helping us find answers to our questions. We learn to expand our intellect and utilise our talents. Adults are also responsible for the unfolding of our sensitivity in our dealings with others and situations: teaching us how to think, to take responsibility for all we do and say, and to allow others to be responsible for themselves. This learning is of the utmost importance.

Unless a child is taught to observe, think and then act, taking responsibility for what it does, it will grow up relying on others to tell it what to do and to sort out its problems and will blame outside sources for its inadequacies.

Once a person becomes aware that they have a choice and takes responsibility, they can realise their own inner strengths and possibilities, allowing the past to be absorbed.

There are many people who are afraid to take this self-responsibility; they find it too great a burden. All their life they have found someone to blame or to whom they could delegate responsibility. Any action, physical, mental or spiritual, that a person takes is theirs. It is placed on their record for self-assessment at a later date when the spirit reunites with its soul. No one can remove a person's life record or take away responsibility from them.

If a person behaves in an irresponsible way, whatever the resons, only they can correct it. If it is not possible to redress the balance in this life, ample opportunity will be available on the spirit's return to its soul. It is not possible to be physically born again to correct a past life imbalance; it is cleared before a new life can begin.

The centre of our existence is the planet earth. Without the planet, there is no soul existence and no spiritual progression. To care for and ensure the physical and therefore spiritual harmony of the earth we have to exist on the same vibration, which is our physical body.

Souls base their main reasons to return to earth, via their spirit energy, on their need to learn and teach, thereby assisting others and the planet. The brain can become so in control that it refuses to allow its spiritual needs to manifest.

Some people refuse to care for the earth while here; they say they are not interested in future generations. If they understood that their energy is part of the future through rebirth, just as it is part of the past, perhaps they would then help right the wrongs which have been inflicted on the earth.

We need balance in our physical and spiritual life whilst on earth. To spend time only on the spiritual aspect of existence is unwise. We are a spirit energy in a physical body, which needs physical energy to keep it well and balanced. The spirit then has a good base to operate from. The well-being of the body and brain are of the utmost importance.

Death

When we reach the end of our time as a physical being, our body dies, the spirit energy cord fades and the spirit is released to return to its soul.

The dying time, chosen before birth, can be fixed to a certain day or planned to occur during a period of time. The way we die is not chosen in advance.

When a crash or disaster occurs, there is a moment of silence immediately afterwards, as though time stands still. This is because all spirits leave their bodies the moment before impact, which can create a hushed, slow motion effect.

After impact, those spirits who are to remain enter their bodies to activate them. Those spirits whose time it is to leave cannot re-enter their bodies and so remain nearby. They are met by spirits of people known to them during their life and their own soul energy.

Many people who have been ill for some time will have been contacted before their dying day and, when the time comes for them to leave, they recognise these spirit friends and feel safe. The spirits of those who die suddenly may need to be soothed, as they can feel shocked and not accept their physical death. The spirit helpers answer their questions and on occasions have to convince them that they have reached the end of their physical life.

When a person dies, those left behind are affected in many ways. Some become very distressed because they arrived too late to say goodbye, could not come for personal reasons or were not informed. Immediately after the spirit has left its body at death it is shown its body at peace. It is given the opportunity to visit those on earth whom it has known and to whom it wishes to say goodbye, and sees the people it loves, whether in the same room or far away.

The spirit of a person who dies in one country can visit, and can be sensed by, a loved one in another country. The room temperature will change, or they may have a dream or sense that the person has died, hearing the news officially at a later date.

Many people get distressed because a loved one appears to have died alone. Some have sat with them, holding their hand and watching their face for hours, but then the moment they leave the room the person dies. When sitting with a dying peron it is important not to breathe intensely or lean over the person whose spirit is trying to leave, as this energises their body and makes it difficult for the spirit to detach with peace. When the watcher leaves the room, their energy fades and the spirit can let go. To help a spirit leave sit quietly next to the dying person and rub their upper back in a clockwise spiral. This will enable the body to relax and the spirit to leave with dignity. If the upper back cannot be rubbed, a hand or foot can be rubbed instead.

When a person dies, those left behind cry and/or grieve because they feel lonely and abandoned, or through relief that a dear one is free from pain and stress. But the freed spirit is not crying: it is going home to its soul. When a person dies, it is the people left behind who experience change and have to adjust.

The way a person dies affects others very deeply. Once the spirit has left the body, it is well cared for and perfectly safe. The physical body is our means of living in the earth's vibration like a purpose-built suit for the duration of the life we have experienced. Once a spirit has left its body, it is not connected at all to that body. In fact, in many cases it is glad to leave it behind and forget the body's limitations.

All people on earth are going through a process of spiritual experience, whether they are aware of it or not. Whatever a person does in their physical life is recorded on the spirit energy and assessed on return to its soul. A soul only has one spirit essence on earth at a time, and the soul is at all times in contact with its spirit essence.

Life's adventure

Living on earth is an adventure. The spirit arrives and makes contact at conception, linking to its earth body in the womb. A spirit who has chosen to stay, and to experience physical life, absorbs life around it. After birth it continues absorbing by touch, smell, sound, sight and taste, gradually building up a record of its own and, via the brain which is also programming, learning and copying all that is sensed and experienced. The preparation for the adventure has begun. The spirit and physical work together with the soul as an observer.

The first years are years of absorbing: the brain and spirit observe everything, gathering as much information as possible about behaviour patterns, environment, survival and communication. We continue to absorb as we grow, learning via parents, guardians, school, college and work, right through to the day when the physical body dies and the spirit returns to its soul, taking the complete record of its own achievements and all that its physical self has been involved in.

We are faced with choice at every step along the path of

life. As humans we need to be aware, make decisions, control and use the brain, and savour each and every experience, dealing with events as they arise. We also have to learn how to say goodbye and let go in situations and relationships and to move through the adventure at a pace which suits us.

When unacceptable energies or events surround us we need to deal with them, and try to understand. We may not like what occurs during some of the adventure, but it is all experience, knowledge and, it is hoped, wisdom. We can learn how to use our physical body as a vehicle, keeping it clean, nourished and dignified. It is how we integrate with life around us that is important.

Striving for goals which are too far in the future is disheartening. If we choose a major goal we need to identify some closer ones more easily attainable to spur us on. Work back from the ultimate goal to see what is needed to make it possible, and plan. Make each step a goal in its own right. These stepping-stone goals allow us to grow and accomplish, whether we reach the final goal or not.

At times life may seem unjust, unfair, cruel, painful or out-of-control. But remember that everything changes constantly, and all things have a use: there is no waste. We are not trapped; we can use our own experience to find a way out of the situation. Each of us has a soul which holds our accumulated experiences from all our lives. Tune in as soon as possible. Seek help if necessary but never feel alone — no one is alone!

When we meet a partner to share our life with, we need to allow them their space. Share experiences. Do not demand; request. If the partnership is unbalanced and unsuitable, know when to let go. Loving is an ongoing caring experience. A good relationship is based on knowing when to make changes.

When we are ready to exchange the gift of love, we need

to make sure the gift is welcome to the person chosen to receive it. Love and care teach us how to give and receive, to be neither possessive nor dismissive. A partnership comprises two people helping each other to grow as spiritual and physical beings, to enjoy living and, by doing so, to help others feel cared for and loved.

We should never underestimate ourselves. The soul has been in existence for aeons. Via its spirit, which is totally its own, it has acquired a wisdom from all its life experiences. When we are living on earth and need inspiration or help, firstly we connect with the record of this life contained in our aura. We then connect with our soul, which is a record of all our experiences from our beginning.

Everyone has to find his or her own path of growth and learning in life. A person who feels he or she has found a way of life should share his or her view but not inflict it on others, remembering he or she does not have the answer for everyone, only for himself or herself at that time.

No one person, way of life, book, religion or philosophy is right for everyone. There are many concepts and theories which contain truths. We should not accept or reject everything that others believe. Investigate and ask questions. Each one of us has our own individual road to follow but we need to learn and select as we travel.

We create our own destiny, each day making a link to the next. By making today the best day we can, the link is strong and clear. While on earth the spirit energy endeavours to improve life around it and to enable all aspects of life to experience the level of dignity and harmony it is capable of achieving.

We need each other in order to survive. We are all part of a vast inter-linking pattern and need to learn to relate to everything around us. All life is connected, whatever form it takes, and a person who tries to isolate himself or herself from others is still affecting, and being affected by, the rest of humanity.

We share all energies, from the air we breathe to our thought patterns. The harmony and disharmony we create become part of that energy and we are all affected. If we each take full responsibility for our contribution through our personal output, in whatever form, this will be the first step towards world-wide harmony and peace.

When we say goodbye to our present life and our spirit returns to its soul, we leave behind memories of ourselves in the minds of others. If we ensure that we leave memories which are inspiring, loving and joyful, we will have contributed to the well-being of the planet, and all on it.

Index